The Secrets of Getting Success in interviews

Author
S Hundiwala

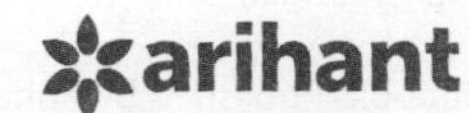

ARIHANT PUBLICATIONS (INDIA) LTD

Arihant Publications (India) Ltd.

卐 Administrative & Production Offices

Regd. Office

'Ramchhaya' 4577/15, Agarwal Road, Darya Ganj, New Delhi -110002
Tele: 011- 47630600, 43518550; Fax: 011- 23280316

卐 Head Office

Kalindi, TP Nagar, Meerut (UP) - 250002
Tele: 0121-2401479, 2512970, 4004199; Fax: 0121-2401648

卐 Sales & Support Offices

Agra, Ahmedabad, Bengaluru, Bhubaneswar, Bareilly, Chennai, Delhi, Guwahati, Hyderabad, Jaipur, Jhansi, Kolkata, Lucknow, Meerut, Nagpur & Pune

卐 ISBN : 978-93-13160-78-6

卐 PRICE : ₹ 145.00

PO No. : TXT-59-T050373-11-22

Published by : Arihant Publications (India) Limited

For further information about books Published by Arihant
log on to www.arihantbooks.com or email to info@arihantbooks.com

Preface

This book 'The Secrets of Getting Success in Interviews' will empower you with the knowledge and skills that will enable you to face interviews with confidence. This book is equally useful for the people who need to sharpen their interviewing abilities.

SPECIAL FEATURES

- The book starts with General Information about Interviews covering Purpose, Objectives and Types of Interviews.
- The book further provides glimpse of the personality traits required for interview. Explanation of each trait is well equipped with an example.
- Guidelines to face interview and interview process are also covered which elaborate preparation of interview in a systematic manner.
- The book has vast coverage of Sample Interviews categorised as Government Sector Interviews, Private Sector Interviews and Admission Interviews. These interviews cover sample interviews for Civil Services, Defence Services, Banking, Railway, Intelligence Bureau, LIC, Marketing Executive, Coordinator, School Teacher, BHM, MBA, Journalism Course, etc.
- It also covers Sample Resumes so that readers can design their resume effectively.
- At the end of the book , some general FAQs are given to familiarise readers with a way of answering common questions in the best possible way.

I am sure this book will certainly be of immense help for the candidates preparing different Interviews.

Wish you best of Luck!

Author

Contents

BASICS ABOUT INTERVIEW

- *Interview : An Introduction*
- *Types of Interview*

The word 'Interview' refers to a one-on-one conversation with one person acting in the role of interviewer and other in the role of interviewee. It is the most important stage of selection in a competitive examination. Here overall personality of a person is judged by an interviewer.

Interview An Introduction

An interview is a conversation between two or more people (the interviewer and the interviewee) where questions are asked by the interviewer to obtain information from the interviewee. In the process of recruitment and selection, interview is probably the most widely used selection tool. Interview is a formal complex mechanism through which the recruiter or organisation is able to find out the most suitable candidate to the jobs for which the interviews are held.

PURPOSE OF AN INTERVIEW

Interviewing is used for a variety of purposes including selection, appraisal, disciplinary action, counselling and general problem solving. It plays an important part both in private and public sector organisation including Civil Services, Defence Services, Banking as well as Paramilitary services. All interviews are held with specific purpose of gathering more information about various qualities or traits of an individual and correlate them with the requirement of the job.

It also helps to verify the quality and accuracy of information obtained through application forms. The interviewer tries to assess a candidates's expression, knowledge, skills and self-confidence from the answers given by the candidate. It offers the employers valuable insight into the candidate's personality and abilities and it also allows the candidate a chance to discern whether his qualifications, aspects and career goals match up with the company's requirement.

OBJECTIVES OF AN INTERVIEW

An interview has different perspective for both employer as well as candidate. Major objectives of interview are

Employer's Perspective

1. **Find Out Your Suitability** The employer or interviewer is interested in finding out how can a candidate contribute to the organisation if he or she is hired. The aim of the interview is to find out how the particular candidate is different or better than the other candidates.
2. **Appearance, Personality and Background** On the basis of interview, empolyer or interviewer also judge your personality traits like-appearance, mannerism, mental alertness, consistency of thought and ideas, leadership qualities etc.
3. **Check the Organisational Fitness of the Candidate** The employers, certainly, would like to check how a candidate will fit in their team, their corporate culture and the organisation itself.
4. **To Check Knowledge and Intelligence of a Candidate** With the help of interview an employer easily check the knowledge and intelligence of a candidate. It includes knowledge of the candidate *wrt* subject of specialisation, applicability of the subject in day-to-day life, knowledge about other general subjects, IQ and common sense etc.
5. **To Promote Goodwill** An interview also gives an opportunity to create and enhance goodwill of the company. The interviewee should be treated with courtesy. If any candidate not selected by the organisation, reasons for the same are explained offering constructive suggestions.

Candidate's Perspective

1. **Suitability of the Job** A candidate must find ways to learn more about the job profile and the responsibilities. A candidate's goal should be whether that particular job will satisfy a candidate's short and long term career goals? A candidate would also check organisation's culture, further growth and opportunity, security of the job etc.
2. **Suitability of Location** With the help of interview a candidate also check about the work location or about the **transferred rule** of transfer if applicable by the organisation.
3. **Remuneration Package** The candidate is always interested to know about remuneration package provided by the organisation for a particular post.

Types of Interview

The basic aim of an interview is to allow an exchange of information between a candidate and the company or organisation through a process of questioning and answering. There are many types of interview which are practised by the interviewer according to their specific requirement.

INTERVIEW BASED ON ORGANISATION

Directed or Structured Interview

Structured interview is also called directed or standardised interview. Such type of interviews are preplanned. In this type of interview, the questions to be asked, the order of the questions, time given to each candidate, the information to be collected from each etc are predecided. Main advantage of such interviews is that they are accurate, non-flexible and precise and are fairly quick to conduct.

Therefore, there will be consistency and minimum bias in such type of interviews. Such interviews make the objectivity more reliable.

The Unstructured Interview

In contrast to structured interview, unstructured interview is more flexible and personal, it is sometimes called informal interviews. In such type of interview, the interviewer has to make a broad evaluation about the candidate i.e. his or her skill, knowledge, interest, attitude etc.

In these interviews, open ended questions are asked to generate qualitative data. This helps the researcher to develop a real sense of a person's understanding of a situation.

The candidate must bear in mind that he should not be casual in such type of interview and try to treat each question with equal importance. These interviews can be time consuming and expensive.

Situational Interview

In situational interviewing job-seekers are asked to respond to a specific situation they may face on the job. These types of questions are designed to draw out more of your analytical and problem-solving skills as well as how you handle problems with short notice and minimal preparation. The key to preparation and success in situational interviews in simply to review your past work experiences and review the steps you took to resolve problems and make corrections.

Stress Interview

The stress interviewing technique is typically used only for positions in which the job-seeker will be facing stress on the job and the interviewer wants to see how well he or she can handle the pressure. The key to surviving stress interviews is to remain clam keep a sense of humor and avoid getting angry or defensive.

INTERVIEW BASED ON MODES OF COMMUNICATION

Telephonic Interview

One of the most convenient and quicker form of interview is telephonic interview. Although, a telephonic interview is relatively straight forward, even highly capable candidates can be rejected at initial stage, but it may also be used at the final stage of the interview. The telephone interview is a tool for the recruiter to assess whether the candidate is a serious applicant and decide whether or not to take him further through the application process.

The question generally asked, focus more on one's general competencies and skills. The candidate must try to show his/her enthusiasm and commitment in a short conversation. In this type of interview you must focus on words you speak, how you speaks, confidence level and the tone in which you speak.

One of the reasons of telephonic interview being so popular is that it is less expensive and time saving procedure. But the candidate should not take these interviews very lightly and should prepare for these as seriously as for a face to face interview.

During or before telephonic interview keep following points in mind

- Keep a copy of the CV and the application form in front of you alongwith a pen and paper.
- Never conduct a phone interview in your car or in a public area because you need to focus all your attention on the interview.
- Always conduct the interview in a quiet private area and ask family members not to distrub you during the interview.
- Never do the following activity like eating, surfing web, text messaging during your telephonic interview.
- Treat your interview as face to face interview.

Personal Interview

This is a one-to-one interview conducted in the form of direct communication. This is one of the most conventional type of interview and it offers an opportunity to the interviewer to assess the candidate by observing body language, voice articulation, facial expression and eye contact. It also gives you an opportunity to establish rapport with interviewers and show them your skills and abilities.

Personal Interview between two people

The interviewer may often have a series of prepared questions but many times an interviewer may also ask questions framed at that time only as the interview progresses and as the situation demands.

The hallmark of a personal interview is that it is typically conducted one on one to observe and conclude whether a particular candidate would be suitable for the company. Personal, does not mean asking very personal questions, the questions may be on individual's working state and experiences. Personal interviews are conducted for market research, admission in a college or for a particular job.

Video-Conference Interview

A midway between a telephonic interview and a face to face interview, video-conferencing is becoming increasingly popular. The video conference interview is exactly what it sounds like : an interview performed long distance by video-conferencing. Such interviews are becoming very common because they save time and money.

Moreover they make it possible to conduct a meeting that otherwise might never occur due to long distance or busy schedule. It gives an employer an opportunity to meet with a candidate using a human like interaction.

Interview being conducted by Video-Conference

Interviewing via video-conferencing can actually be to a candidate's advantage if one can be natural and confident. If a candidate can come in and adapt quickly to this new situation, it reflects very well on the candidate.

During or before video-conference interview keep following points in mind

- Make sure you are facing the webcam. If it is not centered on your computer (perhaps you have two monitors) arrange things such that you are looking at the camera and the interviewer.
- Verify sound levels before the interview.
- Get rid of all distractions on your computer i.e. sign out of chat, close email, etc.
- You can still take notes via paper/pen.
- Turn your phone on silent mode.
- If there are other people in the house at that time, make sure you let them know about the interview and ask them not to enter your room unless there's is an emergency.
- Arrange a replacement communication tool also (e.g. mobile phone) as an alternative.

Written Interview

In this type of interview, the interviewer sends out a form with his/her questions, requesting you to answer them and mail it back to him/her. This type of interview is generally used by research companies or exit poll conducting media/company. The only advantage of this interview is the extended access to participants in comparison to face to face interviews. Another advantage of written interview is that interviewer can formulate the questions at his/her own convenience without noise disturbance. There is no travelling cost involved here.

But there are some disadvantages of this method of interview. This method takes a lot of time. The interviewee might have to wait sometimes for days or weeks before he or she answers the questions. The spontaneous response is also lacking as the interviewee has all the time to give a response after reflecting on the questions for a lot of time. Lack of face to face social cues results in greater cultural and language barriers.

INTERVIEW BASED ON STAGES

First Stage or Screening

First round interviews or screening are typical short and quick interviews aimed at fact-checking, profile matching that a company wants to carry out from a large number of applicants. These interviews are generally taken by middle level HR executive to find out potential candidates for the advanced level. In most cases, this stage includes review of background and list of questions to determine if applicant is fit for the position. This Stage of interviews plays an important part as the interviewer doesn't have to face a candidate lacking basic requirements. It is a cheaper and quicker mode of interview. Their focus is on shortlisting appropriate candidates, who will then continue on to the next round of interviews.

Subsequent Interview

In many organisations, the interview process is not limited to a single round of interview. Multiple interviews are common and may take place due to a number of reasons. The candidate may be called to be interviewed by the key people who were not there in the initial interview. There can be a number of reasons for authorities to hold subsequent interview. These are

- Sometimes, the process of screening is carried over by middle level HR executives or by recruitment agency and subsequent interview is taken by senior officials of the company.
- Sometimes it may happen that interviewers do not reach consensus about the candidate and need to have another look.
- Sometimes different interviewer may test different competencies of an interviewee to make the final selection of the best candidate for the post. e.g. one interviewer might-look at the applicant's technical skills while the other interviewer may assess candidates, behavioural skills or his/her fit in the organisation. Their main aim is to know how well a candidate may be contributing to the team to achieve the company's goals.

INTERVIEW BASED ON NUMBER OF PARTICIPANTS

One-to-One Interview

This interview is confined to an individual at one time. It can be further classified into single interviewee by a single interviewer or individual candidate by a panel of interviewers. This is more like a personal interview where a candidate is assessed for his/her attitudes, beliefs, desires and experiences to get a deeper undertaking of the candidate.

This is the most common type of interview, most useful as it helps in establishing a mutual support and understanding. This method helps in collecting sufficient information as the interviewer may be asked questions related to a wide variety or aspects. Attitudes, feelings opinion etc can be successfully evaluated and analysed through individual interviews but this method is time consuming.

One-to-One Interview between a single interviewee and a single interviewer

Panel or Board Interview

In this type of interview, the candidate is interviewed by more than two individuals in a group. This is one of the most common form of interview and is normally held at final selection stages or for senior appointments. Each member of the panel brings a different set of experience, thoughts beliefs and biases to the interview process.

Panel or Board Interview between a single interviewee and a panel

Panel interviews are often characterised by a standard set of questions for all applicants. Panel interviews are becoming increasingly common as the job market hots up and companies look for more rigorous ways to screen job seekers and spot the best talent.

Often uncomfortable for a candidate, panels save organisation's time, particularly if company is recruiting people for a number of positions in various departments.

Group Interview

This type of interview is opposite to panel interview. Instead of several interviewers and one candidate, one interviewer will sometimes interview several candidates at the same time. Purpose of group interview is to identify a 'leader' among participants. This type of interview is not very effective and used rarely in the organisation.

Group Interview between a panel and many interviewees

INTERVIEW BASED ON OTHER ASPECTS

Campus Interview

A lot of companies rush to prestigious colleges to recruit the best fresh out of college talents available every year. This is called campus interview.

In the campus interview the company is at the door step of the candidate and lined up to recruit the best among them. As the candidates are all freshers, the interviewer keeps it in mind that these people do not have any or marginal experience of working in an office.

Position interviewed are generally entry-level in nature and encompass a broad range of functional areas including finance, marketing, management, sales, operations, social service, engineering and technology.

Technical Interview

Technical interviews are specific interviews for technical jobs. Mostly people with adequate experience are invited and questions related to technical know how are asked.

The technical heads of any organisation may interview the concerned individual, may ask detailed questions about specific technologies, development theory problem solving approach and a host of other topics.

A candidate is interviewed on the basis of practical questions designed to measure his analytical abilities and his command over the practical/ technical aspect of the job. The recruiter may like to know how well versed a candidate is with ever changing technologies in his domain and how relevant his knowledge will be for on going or future needs of the company.

However assessing technical knowledge will not be the only point of the interview. The company or the interviewer might try to look at candidates' problem solving ability i.e. how you think and how importantly one communicates one's thinking during the interview.

GENERAL INTERVIEW STRUCTURES

Interview is different from an informal type of conversation. Different types of interview follow a different procedures in which some set of questions are asked from the candidate. These set of questions may be different for private jobs, government jobs, admission time questions, questions generally relate to practical aspect of interviews.

Keeping in mind the specific purpose, the interviewers select the interview structure that may best fulfil their specific requirement. We will discuss about structures of three main areas

1. Public or Government Sector Interview
2. Private Sector Interview
3. Admission Interview at the time of admission into college/institutes such as technical institutes or business schools.

Private Sector Job Interviews

The purpose of job interview in the private sector is to choose the most suitable candidate for specific post. Whether it is a technical post or managerial post a standard format is practised.

In private sector, interview can be done through following ways.

- The interview may be taken by an individual or a group of interviewers but they all follow a standard pattern.
- The interviewer may ask some casual questions to build a rapport and try to make the candidate feel better at the initial stage. It can also be called opening the interview with ice-breaking questions.

Some sample questions which an interviewer may ask during an interview

- Did you have a good journey?
- I hope you could find the address easily.

The interviewer will often start the main part of the interview by asking an open question such as 'would you describe your current responsibilities to me?' or 'would you give me a rundown of your current post'?

If a CV of a candidates contains career breaks or period of unemployment in between, question will be asked about these such as what were you doing when you were not employed? The question will be person specific and will differ from one individual to another.

The interviewer closes the interview and asks the candidate to follow whatever steps are there in the selection process. Before leaving candidate must thank the interviewer and wish them.

Public or Government Sector

The public sector follows its own definite prescribed order in which an interview is held. Generally government jobs interviews are more or less personality test which try to ascertain a candidates' ability to adapt himself to a particular situation or his leadership qualities, balanced opinion or power of judgement.

In such type of interview questions may be asked in a directed and purposive manner to find out candidate's mental abilities, his general knowledge and awareness as well as his depth of knowledge. How well he will be able to apply his knowledge is also tested.

- Possible questions on the home town, state or birthplace or year can be asked.
- Question related to the main subject of study and application of knowledge in the modern scenario can be asked.
- The interviewer may ask questions related to hobbies and extra-curricular activities.

- Question related to national or international major current events or other burning topics may be asked. Questions related to social, cultural or financial (economical) problem and possible solutions will also be asked.

The main difference in private and government jobs interview questions is that in private sector questions related to a person's key skills, positive or negative attitude, team spirit, devotion to job and career growth are asked.

Admission Interviews

Interviews are also held for school or college students who try to claim a seat in the professional courses of various institutions or universities. The interviewer look for candidates with skill sets and intellectual and analytical skills. For admission to a business school the interviewer may try to find out candidates with good leadership qualities, communication skills and confident outlook.

Generally following steps are followed during admission interview

- A written test is conducted to reduce the number of qualified student.
- Only meritorious students are called for interview and group discussions.

A candidate is finally selected keeping in mind his performance in written tests, group discussions and rounds of personal interviews clubbed together. Every institute have their own set of parameters on which a candidate is selected.

ESSENTIAL PERSONALITY TRAITS

- *Presonality Traits Required for Interview*
- *Preparation before Interview*
- *Appearing for the Interview*
- *The Interview Process*
- *Post Interview Activity*

Personality is one of the important attributes to acquire success in your career. With the help of incorporating essential personality traits and preparing well, one can perform best in his/her interview.

Personality Traits Required for Interview

Personality is the unique combination of patterns that influence behaviour, thought, motivation and emotion in a human being. The term 'Personality' has been defined in many ways but as psychological concept two main meanings have evolved.

One is that personality is everything that makes you an individual. *Second*, it is important to keep in mind that the culture in which we live is one of the most important environmental factors that shape our personalities.

One must remember that knowledge of subject and general studies are only one important aspect of interview, how an interviewee presents himself, his way of talking, appearance, mannerism all are equally important.

APPEARANCE

An interviewer not only judges a person on the basis of his knowledge and ideas but on an overall personality. The way one appears or dresses up leaves a great effect on others specially the interviewer.

Interviewer assesses your appearance at interview, considers your way of dressing, accessories etc. Sometimes interviewer asked the question related to your appearance.

EXAMPLE

(Questions related to candidate's appearance & attire)

Chairman How are you Mr. Peter? You are looking very smart specially the colour of your shirt.

Candidate Thank you Sir.
- (Your answer should be spontaneous without any nervousness)

Chairman Your tie appears to be new. Did you buy it for this interview?

Candidate No Sir, this is six months old. I rarely wear this. This is a gift from my elder brother.

Chairman Mr. Peter your shirt is going well with matching pair of trousers. Your choice of clothes is really nice.

Candidate Thank you Sir. I am very careful in colour combinations. I make sure that I wear proper and matching combinations. I am thankful for your appreciation.

NOTE *Here please note that Mr. Peter has performed above average in this part of interview as he managed to answer instantly without any trace of nervousness and hesitation.*

MANNERISM

The interview consists of a number of dialogues or verbal responses, which serve as a means of communicating one's ideas. It is true that a man's linguistic style is a mirror that reflects his personality, one should keep in mind to speak clearly without any hesitation and perfect modulation to leave a good impression on the interviewer. One should show basic courtesies during an interview such as greeting your interviewer, keeping your mobile phone on silent mode, etc.

EXAMPLE

(Questions to show how a candidates confidence level and basic countries help in tackling interview questions)

Chairman Hello, Miss Sujatha.

Candidate Good Morning Sir.

Chairman You are late for this interview. Aren't you?

Candidate (Smiling) Speaks in a courteous manner. No Sir, I am well in time. As soon as my name was announced, I headed for this room. (Mark polite but confident way of speaking)

Chairman Please take your seat.

Candidate (Takes a chair meant for candidate and sits without making any noise) Thank you very much Sir.

Chairman Looking at your documents, I believe that you have graduated from Meerut University. This University is not very reputed for imparting knowledge. Moreover, atmosphere is very disturbing. What is your opinion?

Candidate (Speaks in a moderate tone, but makes a direct eye contact with the Chairman) I beg to differ from your opinion Sir. I have studied in this University for 3 years. I had taken part in many extra curricular activities like seminars, symposium and inter-college debate competitions, which taught me so much beside gaining knowledge in the subjects of graduation. I am thankful to my lecturers of my university who are role models for me. I am proud to be part of this university and I did not find the atmosphere disturbing.

NOTE *She praises her lecturers very smartly, points towards participating in extra curricular activities showing that University atmosphere is cordial and congenial to learning.*

COMMUNICATION SKILLS

Effective communication is the basic prerequisite of attaining organisational goals. It is expected that the candidate possesses reasonably good communication skills. This skill is much more than mere articulation as it includes listening and logical sequencing of statements. During an interview, a candidate is judged on the basis of his communication skill also. Employers seek employees who can get along with others and have ability to communicate both verbally or non-verbally.

EXAMPLE

(Example showing effective communication skills)

Chairman Good morning Mr. Vivek.

Candidate Good morning Sir.

Chairman Mr. Vivek we would like to know how well you other people.

Candidate Sir, I am a patient listener and good communicator, which is essential to being a sales representative. Customers often call me with their complaints and concerns and my ability to patiently listen and empathise makes them feel appreciated. Then I try to come up with a solution on to their problem.

NOTE *How well the candidate has shown the interviewers his communication skill ability through which he is able to solve people's problems.*

MENTAL ALERTNESS

One important personality trait is mental alertness and consistency which shapes a person's personality. This alertness refers to candidate's understanding of the question put to him/her in the minimum time possible. The Interview Board tests the mental alertness of the candidate through different ways by asking confusing questions, interrupting when the candidate is trying to put across his point of view or throwing a number of questions one after another without giving much time to the candidate to answer the questions. For the development of mental alertness one should concentrate and give attention toward details. At the same time for presence of mind, intensive observation power should be there in candidate.

EXAMPLE

(Example showing mental alertness of the candidate)

Candidate May I please come in, Sir?

Chairman Yes, come in Mrs. Nayyar.

Candidate Thank you and good morning to you all.

Chairman What is good about morning Mrs. Nayyar? It is quite warm and there is nothing special about this morning.

Another nterviewer How did you come to this place? What was the time when you reached here at the reception?

Candidate Without showing any signs of nervousness, (smiles and says), Sir, let me first answer first question. Sir, the time is to wish good morning. As far as the goodness of this morning is concerned, I must say, the atmosphere inside the room is very pleasant and comfortable. Now let me answer the second question Sir.

NOTE *See her alertness, she has not forgotten to answer the second question while answering first one. I reached here at the reception at8 : 42 am Sir.*

Chairman How do you know it was 8 : 42?

Candidate Sir, I am in habit of looking at my watch wherever I go. Moreover, my interview time was 9 am and I wanted to be here 10 or 15 minutes before interview starts. So, I checked my watch Sir.

Chairman Ok, I think it is a good habit to reach anywhere a few minutes before time.

NOTE *The Chairman and the interruption by other interviewer were meant to only confuse the candidate. But the answers given by the candidate are worth praising.*

CONSISTENCY OF THOUGHTS AND IDEAS

Consistency is related to alertness of mind. Maturity in thinking, being practical and not driven by sentiments, emotions or external forces and having practical attitude. Sometimes the process of interview can be long and drawn out. Consistency of thoughts and ideas is incredibly very important in such situations. The interview board tries to judge the candidate's consistency by asking the same question in the beginning and repeating it later in a different form at the later stage of an interview. One should not change one's opinion even when one is induced by the interviewer to do so. Being consistent requires all powers of concentration. Consistency is also required in temper and action on the part of the candidate. A candidate should not try to contradict himself or his opinions in the influence of others. This reflects his immaturity lack of consistency.

EXAMPLE

(Example showing consistency of thoughts)

Candidate May I come in Sir.

Chairman Yes, Mr. Vijay Dube, you may come in please.

Candidate (Walks confidently towards the Board's table and smilingly wishes to all board members) Good Morning, Sir.

Chairman Good Morning Mr. Dube, please be seated.

Candidate Thank you Sir.

Chairman Mr. Dube I see from your academic record that you had secured good marks in social science and economics right from your High School. What is your favourite subject?

Candidate Yes Sir, Economics is my favourite subject.

Chairman Do you think Mr. Dube that black money is responsible for the present economic condition of our country?

Candidate Yes Sir, black money is responsible for the present economic crisis in India.

Chairman What about the step taken by PM Modi to curb the problem of black money? Didn't it exploit common masses more?

Candidate No Sir, common masses do not have large amount of money, so the problem is with the politicians and officials who take large amount of money as a bribe, for that they do not pay any tax.

NOTE *In the above example, the candidate has depicted his consistency and firm stand on the issues under discussion. His politeness in answers is worth praising.*

ATTITUDE

As soon as candidate enteres in building, the interview starts. Being on time, way of talking to receptionist, and the most important after the initial entry, hand shake or saying good morning. A candidate has to keep the right impression going throughout the interview. During the process of answering of questions one has to be confident, enthusiastic, responsive and energetic as well as interested, alert and showing positive attitude.

A person's facial expressions as well as his answers reflect a lot. One's pleasant manner and smile while answering shows a relaxed attitude. Never criticise, never complain about your previous job. Talk about what can you do, not what you can't do. One should never underestimate oneself. Always try to say or show that you will be able to meet the challenge in spite of hardships or difficulty level.

EXAMPLE

(Example showing positive attitude of a candidate)

Chairman Please be seated Mr. Dinesh.

Candidate Thank you so much Sir (Takes a chair without much noise and sits relaxed but alert.)

Chairman Mr. Dinesh why should we hire you for this position i.e. 'Senior Manager'?

Candidate (Displaying interest in the job) From what I understand you want someone who can efficiently handle the office administration, communicate with the workers and do coordination with the Head Office. I have experience in almost all administration related areas. Apart from the usual administration tasks, I also have been checking the purchase requirement and coordinating and following up with vendors. I hope it will help me do this job efficiently.

NOTE *Here the candidate's positive attitude is clearly seen in his statements. He is willing to take up any challenge that may come in his job and use his experience to solve problems.*

EXAMPLE

(Example showing negative attitude of the candidate)

Chairman Please be seated Mr. Dinesh.

Candidate Thank you Sir (Looks around to see where he can sit and takes too much time to settle down.)

Chairman How was your journey from Amritsar to Delhi? I hope you could find this place comfortably.

Candidate No Sir, my journey was quite troublesome. My seat was not reserved so I came in a bus which took too much time. Moreover, this place was new to me so I had to stop and ask many people about this present venue.

NOTE *The conversation throws light on the negative attitude of the candidate as he was late in getting reservation done. He has not bothered to find out the venue before hand or take the directions from somebody. This also reflects that may be he was not very keen for attending this interview.*

SELF-CONFIDENCE

The term 'Self-Confidence' means a belief in one self. A belief that one can do a task as one has self-belief. It is a key trait of a balanced personality as it encourages you to be free of doubts and fears. Self-confidence can contribute a lot towards a person's better personal and professional life.

In order to develop self-confidence it is necessary that a person should be able to overcome his fears and doubts. Fear just adds to nervousness and stress and person is not able to think logically under stress or doubts.

One should try to be courageous and have conviction of belief, than only one can succeed. A positive attitude helps in gaining self-confidence.

Strong will power is another factor to achieve self-confidence. To gain confidence one should set realistic goal, should have knowledge of personal strengths and weaknesses.

EXAMPLE

(Example showing self confidence of the candidate)

Candidate	May I come in, Sir.
Chairman	Yes Mr. Devesh Verma, come in and take your seat.
Candidate	Thank you Sir (Sits down and appears relaxed.)
Chairman	Well, Mr. Devesh, we had forgotten to inform you that the job will include an additional, but important duty that was not mentioned in the job profile.
Candidate	(Still relaxed and enthusiastic) No problem Sir that's fine with me Sir. I am used to taking on new duties and I love challenges.
Chairman	Well, Mr. Devesh, what is your feeling about achieving success in this interview?
Candidate	Sir, I am sure to come out successful. I have worked hard for this. (Note the speaker's confidence)
Another Member	Suppose we reject you now, will you take a second chance.
Candidate	Madam, first of all, I think I am not going to be rejected. However, if it does happen, I will try again and again.

NOTE *The answers of this candidate here depict his self-confidence and determination. Even at the mention of additional duty, he does not show any anger or dismay. He is sure of success and he is also willing to try many times until he becomes successful. All these qualities show candidates' boldness, confidence in his abilities and face new challenges.*

APPLICATION OF KNOWLEDGE AND SUBJECT

A candidate's academic knowledge and ability to utilise or apply that knowledge in day to day work is an essential personality traits that is tested in an interview. The candidate must have a good subject knowledge and general knowledge. One must learn to adapt oneself with flexibility of one's skills, the job title or duties.

Interviewer want to find out how you think and apply your current knowledge to unfamiliar problems. A whole new world of career opportunities can open up if the candidate can understand that skills and related knowledge are of prime importance and can be developed with practise.

If one is knowledgeable and apply that knowledge in replying different types of questions, it will not be difficult to come out a winner in an interview. To improve subject knowledge one must read the newspaper daily, read magazines and articles etc.

EXAMPLE

(Example showing application of knowledge)

Chairman Hello, Mr Vivek, take you seat please.

Condidate Good morning sir and thank you.

Chairman I see from your application form that you belong to Punjab and most of your life has been spent in this part of the country. Why do you think, Punjab is prospering as compared to other states ever with the problem of terrorism?

Candidate Sir, it is a farm-oriented state. The farmers of Punjab are very hard working and use technology in farming. Soil and climatic conditions are also favourable. All these factors together are responsible for the prosperity in Punjab.

Chairman Mr. Vivek, here I disagree with you. There are lots of industries in Punjab, take the case of Ludhiana, for example.

Candidate Sir, No doubt industries too play a vital role in Punjab's progress. But 80% people of Punjab still live in villages and are engaged in farming. We cannot deny the farming community's contribution in the state's overall progress.

NOTE *In this interview, the candidate knows his subject well and discusses the issues related to his state in a clear and concise manner but in a polite tone.*

LEADERSHIP ATTRIBUTES

A good leader possesses the talents needed to be an efficient manager, exemplifies the qualities of a good worker and motivates others to imitate those traits. This is an important personality trait which is required in an organisation or company where a person has to lead a team of workers. A good leader is able to recognise and effectively balance the interests and needs of one's own group with those of the broader organisation.

He should be able to build trust with others through own authenticity and follow through on commitments. Work force or team are more willing to pursue a leader whose deeds represent what his words articulate. Good communication skill, decisiveness, confidence in own abilities, positive attitude, team spirit, politeness, givedue credit are the some qualities of good team leader.

EXAMPLE

(Example showing leadership qualities of a candidate)

Candidate Good Morning Sir.

Chairman Good Morning, Mr. Dutt, please be seated.

Candidate Thank you Sir (takes seat very efficiently)

Chairman Well, Mr. Dutt you have applied for the post of Sr. Manager (operations) why do you believe you would make a good manager?

Candidate I think Sir a good manager is able to lead, for example, motivate his team and develop potential team leaders. I believe I would make a good manager because of my ability to lead from the front and be a good listener within the past two years. I have been able to motivate my team and finish the project before the set dead lines.

Chairman Can you elaborate how did you manage to deal with difficult people in your team?

Candidate Sir, there was one difficult person in the team. Though she was good at her work she wanted to show that she was a much better performer. She used to withheld information which she should have tried to share with the rest of the team. It created a lot of problem in the functioning of the team and the work.

Chairman How were you able to sort out this problem?

Candidate I talked to her and tried to find out why she was not working together with the team. I told her the difficulties which we were facing due to her attitude. After 2 sittings, she was able to understand the problem and started cooperating and sharing the information with others. She had one objection. She told me that many times others also did not share the information with her. I had talks with other members of team also and told them the importance of working together rather than showing individual talent.

NOTE *Here the candidate is able to visualise the problem. He is also able to change the individual's behaviour whose non-cooperating attitude was affecting the working of the whole team, like a good leader.*

Preparation Before An Interview

When a candidate is called for an interview, he or she must start practicing from the same day to the actual day of interview. Planning and preparing for the interview will give the confidence to handle a situation and come out with flying colours. There are many steps which have to be followed while preparing for the interview.

Research the Company

The foremost preparation to be done is to acquaint oneself with the organisation. A recent survey confirmed that employers complain about one most common job deficiency among the candidates is that they do not know enough about the organisation or the company.

They should never ever walk into an interview without knowing the company and its products, problems, opportunities and competitors. Employers show interest in candidates who pose intelligent questions and indulge in striking conversation with the interviewer based on their knowledge about the organisation. While a candidate is preparing for an interview, he or she should try to find out all relevant details (about products and services) about the company from its website.

Some facts which should be researched by the candidate prior to going for actual interview are

- About the product and services provided by the organisation.
- About management and history of the company.
- What is the location of the company?
- Who are company's major competitors?

- Go through opinion of clients, vendors and competitors about the company.
- Find out significant trends in that particular industry.
- Find out recent media reports about the company, if any.

A candidate must have a reasonably good knowledge of what the job profile requires. If a person is applying for an executive post, one must do everything to find out about the organisation, its executive body including details on the CEO etc.

Keep Ready All the Documents

Go through your resume minutely a day before interview and keep current resume and coverletter with you. This will enable a candidate to answer all kinds of questions related to educational qualifications and experience etc. One day before an interview prepare a folder where all your documents including marksheets, certificates should be arranged in a chronological order. One may be asked to reproduce the same for verification.

Keep interview call letter at the top in your folder. Be sure you know exactly where the location of interview is and how much commuting time it takes to get there.

Confidence Boost up

Success occurs when preparation meets opportunity. Preparation is required in all walks of life. Facing an interview may be a daunting task, but it is also not difficult as many people may think. Performing well at an interview requires correct preparation, a little practise, proper attitude and lots of confidence.

Boosting of confidence can be done through various ways. Some of them are

Improve Your Rapport Building Skills

Rapport is a state of harmonious understanding with another individual or group that enables easier communication. Building and maintaining rapport is important for employer also as because without good rapport there is lack of credibility and trust, if these two things are absent there will be no true communication and good rapport will also help interviewer to group relevant information. One should remember that first few seconds of an interview are very important in impressing the interviewer. A pleasant smile may help a person establish an instant relationship with people. Communication plays an important part in building rapport and trust.

Learn to Speak Positive Statements

A candidate must remember that a positive attitude can go a long way in making a lasting and positive impression. People or company want knowledgeable but happy, friendly people. Most employers want people who are open, easily accessible and communicative. One should also be able to volunteer positive information about oneself and one's abilities.

A person who shows positive attitude in accepting a responsibility or role is likely to come out a winner. One must say that he is flexible, knows a great deal about the company, he or she is a team player and is highly motivated. A candidate must prepare how he would make such positive statements along with elaborations if he is asked to do so. Never say something to criticise your previous job or boss.

Learn to Handle Difficult and Odd Questions

All the interviewers at one stage or the other ask question which are very confusing or bizarre. They are asked to judge a candidates' mental alertness and consistency in thinking and behaviour. The candidate must prepare well to handle such difficult or odd questions.

Should never answer in mono syllables of 'Yes' or 'No' or if the interviewer asks why do you want to leave the present job one must be well prepared to answer this question. Confusing questions can even be tactic to see how a job seeker thinks about a problem, one must prepare well how to answer such off shoot questions as it is a skill to answer such questions instead of to be taken aback.

Try to Overcome Your Anxiety

As soon as a candidate gets an interview call, signs of nervousness can be seen on his face. It is natural to feel nervous or having anxiety about a job interview. Pre interview anxiety can really sabotage a candidates' performance on the day of interview. A bad case of nervousness can lead to serious interview mistakes including blanking out, blurting, babbling, sweating etc. One has to be prepared well to overcome all these signs of anxiety and nervousness.

If prepared well, one can overcome anxiety with confidence. This confidence can help a person to channelise one's nervous energy into a positive force. There are many ways to overcome anxiety such as taking simple deep breath, being confident and having positive attitude.

ESSENTIAL SKILL REQUIRED FOR AN INTERVIEW

Body Language

Our body postures can speak a silent language that can tell a lot about a candidate. Interviewers make their first impression about a candidate from his personal appearance. Body language makes the decision more concrete. The interview is a type of psychoanalysis of the candidate through which his maturity, emotional stability, tact, self-confidence, initiative, conscientiousness, integrity, consistency of thought, adaptability and ability to work in a team are observed and assessed. With practise one can have enough control over body postures.

Some gestures that leave a positive impression include

1. Sit upright but not too stifly in chair, show a relaxed posture, keeping back straight.
2. Give a normal hand shape but not for a long time.
3. Smiling while expressing thanks or on being appreciated.
4. Speak confidently.
5. Nodding of head while the interviewer is talking to show that you are actively listening.
5. Direct eye contact but do not stare aggessively.
6. Walk confidently and stand firmly and squarely.
7. Keeping a sober expression if the topic is serious.

Some gestures that leave a negative impression and should be avoided are

1. Avoiding eye contact and looking down.
2. Be inaudible and mumble.
3. Fiddling with hands or biting of nails.
4. Ignore other person's presence.
5. Having arms crossed (shows defiance).
6. Slump in front of people or slouch.

7. Shaking one's legs while sitting or answering a question.
8. Raising of eyebrows to show surprise.
9. Waving of hands and arms can be perceived as uncertainty and lack of professionalism.

Speech Articulation

While preparing for the interviewer one must remember that the tone of voice is very important factor in an interview. One should not be in a habit of whispering or speaking very softly so that he may be asked to repeat himself, do not speak too slowly so that you are pausing among words indeed pause between sentences. One must practise to speak at a moderate speed, as some people just rush through their sentences as if they are in a hurry to leave the place. One must remember that during interview he/she needs to be articulate, audible and logical. One should also do away with face actions specially if it is inconsistent.

One must focus on building ample vocabulary and practice correct pronunciation. This is one of the key competency that the interviewers look for in a candidate.

Honesty and Integrity in Self-Description

One must practise to be honest about one's achievement, professional qualification and work experience etc. Lying about one's strengths and work can cause distress in future, so candidate need to be honest about his self-description.

If one lacks integrity and honesty, chances of damaging oneself become higher and damage a candidate's chance of being selected? While describing about work experience or skills, a person should be honest and correct in providing information. While talking about past failures one should be honest about one' mistakes. At the same time practise to comment about what one has learnt out of those mistakes.

SKILL ENHANCEMENT

Listening and Communication Skill

It is very essential for any prospective candidate to prepare good listening and communication skills. It is important to note that listening is a good habit. One must prepare to be patient and learn to listen attentively to what others are saying one cannot answer correctly if one does not listen property. A little practise or preparation can go a long way in making an interview a success. Equally important is good communication which includes both content and delivery. People with effective interpersonal communication skills demonstrate a range of behaviours that make the people interact comfortably and bring harmony to the work place. An interviewer certainly tries to assess a candidate on these skills as they are a must to maintain a happy and productive work place. So often the interviewer asks a question about 'How do you deal with an angry person at work'? So a candidate must prepare to come out with a proper answer.

Cooperation with Others or Team Spirit

An interviewer would certainly ask questions from the candidate whether he is a team player or he wants to work alone. The candidate must prepare himself to answer such questions as would you like to be a part of some team or do you want to be alone while working? The candidate must answer this question in a diplomatic way that he would be comfortable both ways—working with a group or working on his own and exploring new things. Such preparations really come handy while answering and you can show that you are competent to work and cooperate in a team.

Effective Planning Skills

It is very difficult to imagine a job where planning and organising skills are not involved. Even the technology has largely taken over many of routine tasks performed by people in the past but most jobs these days involve a lot of planning and organising. There are certain other skills which are involved in making a person perfect planner. A candidate must pay attention and mention these while answering questions related to planning. Analysing and interpreting data and situation, diagnosing problem and identifying its causes predicting and forecasting, goal setting and deciding possible courses of actions communicating, listening, patience and of course knowledge.

Ability to Work Under Stress

All types of jobs involve some degree of pressure whether it is hitting targets, working to deadlines or managing multiple tasking. Having the ability to work to the best of your ability while under considerable pressure is something that all employers look for so it is important that candidate prepares for questions related to this and also have some examples to show that he is capable of dealing with such situations. To deal with such situations one should nottry to control uncont rollable, prioritise tasks, create balance schedule and last but not the least initiating positive relationship.

Ability to Handle Difficult Situation

In almost every job interview question that is asked there will be an endeavour to evaluate a candidate if he is the most suitable one for this position. Generally an interviewer asks question about challenging experiences one had in his professional life and the difficult situation that a candidate has faced in his previous job. These questions are asked to evaluate his/her problem solving ability and analytical skills. Candidate must prepare and try to remove difficult work situations that he may have experienced in his previous work or during internship. A candidate must illustrate the situation, how he used his skills to analyse the problem. Also try to explain the solution which was selected by him or the final outcome of his efforts.

Improve Your Presentation Skills

A presentation is means of communication which can be adapted to various situation where one has to convey some message such as boardroom meeting, briefing team. An interviewer can ask a candidate about his competencies and he might ask to demonstrate his competent skills. So candidate while appearing for an interview must prepare or think about a presentation which he might have to give in front of the interviewers.

Probable Questions Preparation

Questions asked during interviews are the tools used by the interviewer to determine a candidate's knowledge, his personality traits and behaviours, candidate's area of specialisation and their applicability and the level of their general awareness in order to determine their suitability for the job.

Note *Some common questions which are generally asked during an interview are given in next section.*

INTERVIEW

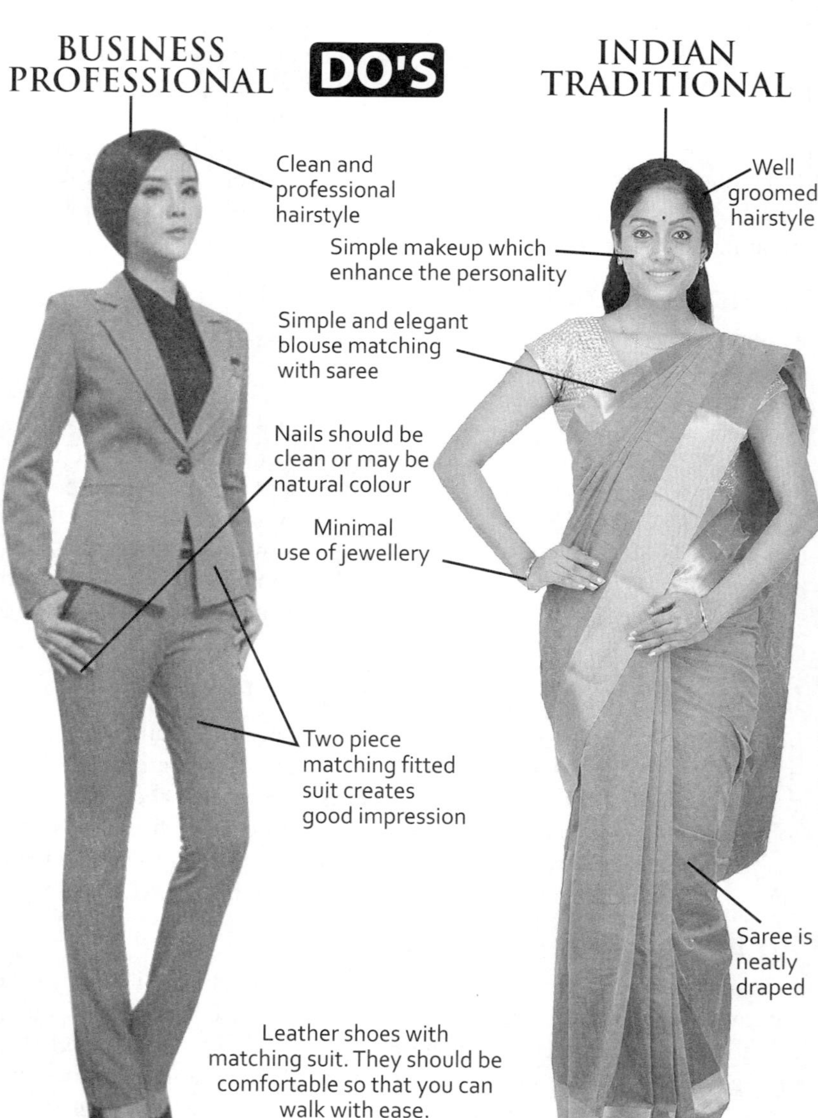
BUSINESS PROFESSIONAL
DO'S
INDIAN TRADITIONAL
Clean and professional hairstyle
Well groomed hairstyle
Simple makeup which enhance the personality
Simple and elegant blouse matching with saree
Nails should be clean or may be natural colour
Minimal use of jewellery
Two piece matching fitted suit creates good impression
Saree is neatly draped
Leather shoes with matching suit. They should be comfortable so that you can walk with ease.

OUTFITS (FEMALE)

TIP

- Check yourself in the mirror before leaving the house.
- Don't have excessive body odour or perfume.
- Don't have your phone on loud tone mode.

INTERVIEW

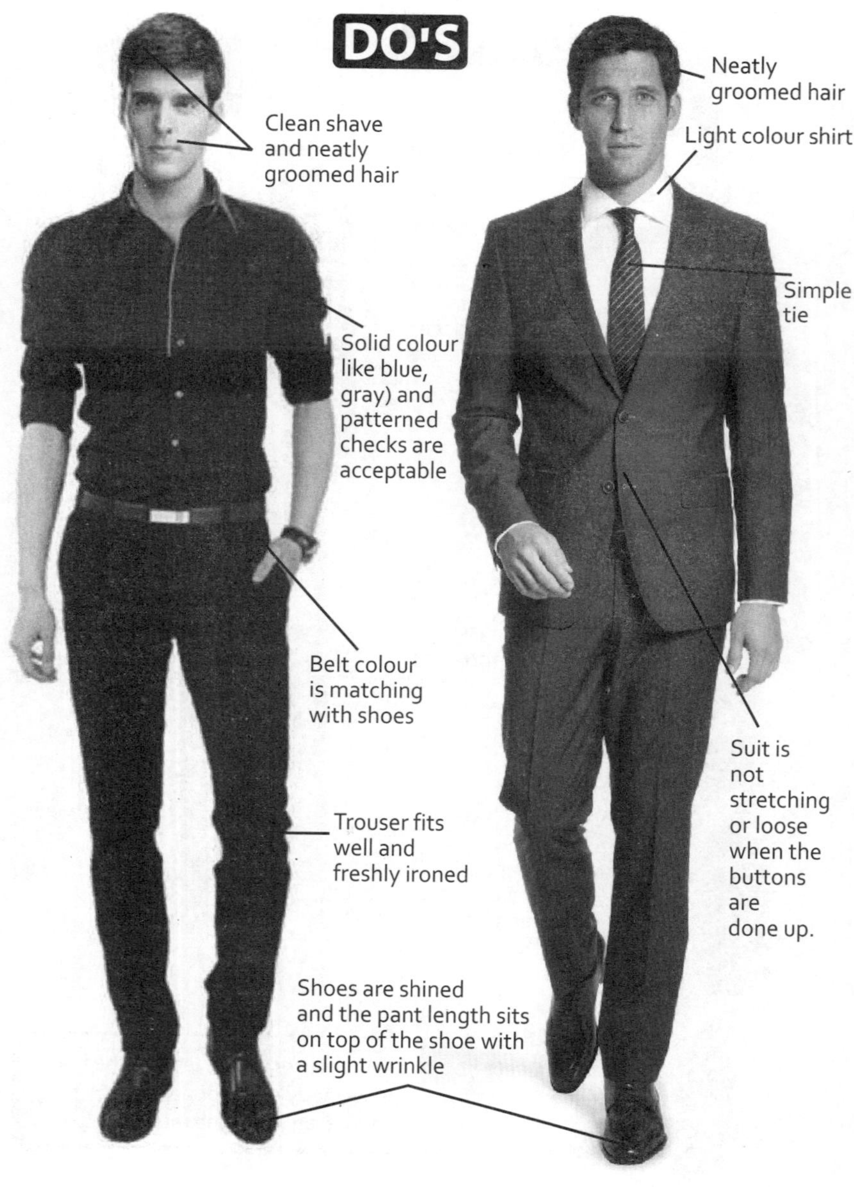
DO'S
Clean shave
and neatly
groomed hair
Neatly
groomed hair
Light colour shirt
Simple
tie
Solid colour
like blue,
gray) and
patterned
checks are
acceptable
Belt colour
is matching
with shoes
Suit is
not
stretching
or loose
when the
buttons
are
done up.
Trouser fits
well and
freshly ironed
Shoes are shined
and the pant length sits
on top of the shoe with
a slight wrinkle

OUTFITS (MALE)

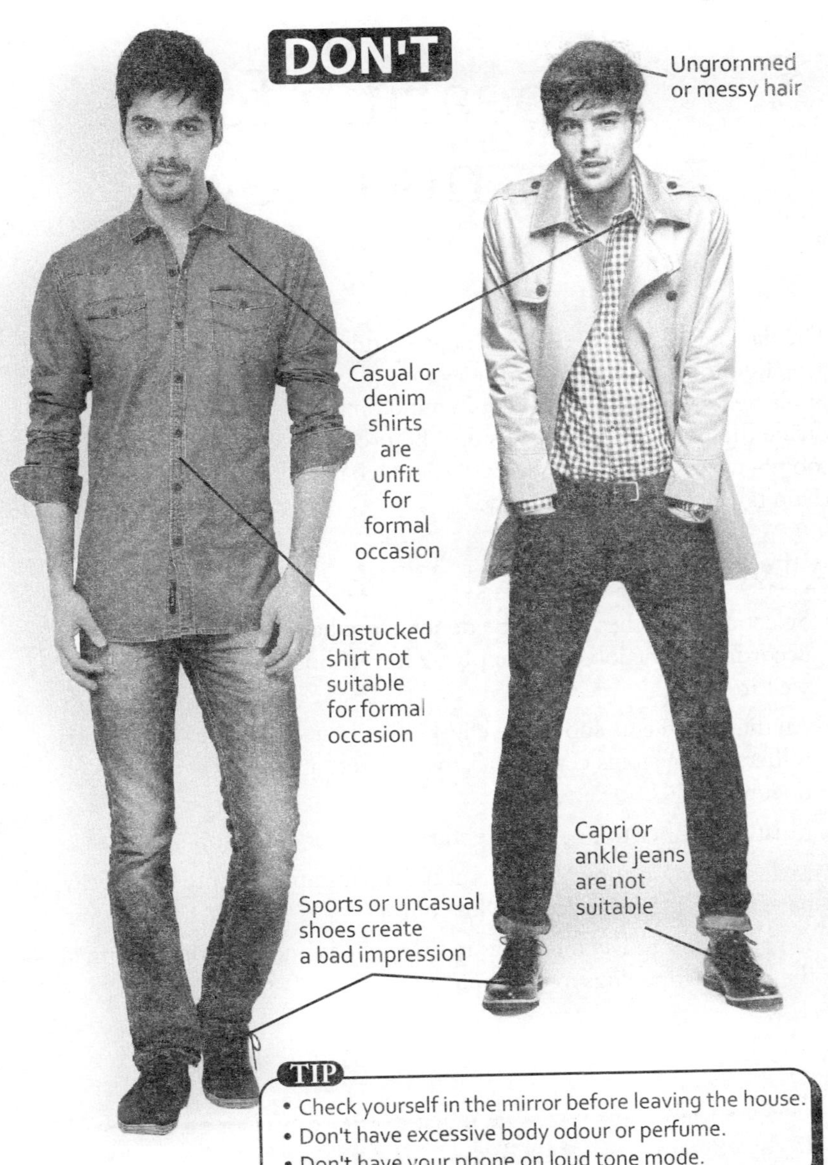

TIP

- Check yourself in the mirror before leaving the house.
- Don't have excessive body odour or perfume.
- Don't have your phone on loud tone mode.

Appearing for the Interview

The day of interview is certainly an eventful one. While a candidate has prepared for the job interview questions, there are certain basic etiquettes or elements which must be kept in mind on the day of interview. We may divide these elements in three steps. Before interview, inside the interview room—what should be done (Do's) and what should not be done (Don'ts) and after the interview.

A DAY BEFORE THE INTERVIEW

- Selection of clothes should be done before hand. Choose the dress according to the job one is applying for. It should be clean and well-ironed.
- All the documents should be checked and the candidate should carry a folder having all his certificates, mark sheets and other necessary documents.
- Must remember to put the interview call letter at the top of folder.
- Make sure your knowledge about the organisation is upto date and you have all the requisite details with you.
- Do not forget to listen to news in the night as one should be aware of the latest happenings in the country.

ON THE DAY OF THE INTERVEIW

- To avoid any unpleasant situation or unnecessary panic, make scene to get ready in time to take all the required document with you.

Reaching on Time

- One of the most important factor that counts a lot in an interview is to reach at the interview venue in time. Some people reach very early and some reach late. Both the situations are not appreciated. Some people reach very early and pester the staff or front desk executive to remind the interviewer that they are already in. This can be very irritating and annoying for the front disk personel or the interviewer. Surveys have revealed that if a candidate is late even by a few minutes, he is usually not considered for the interview.
- Ideally one should try to arrive at the venue about fifteen minutes before his/her scheduled time so that if there is any formality to be done before interview starts, it can be completed. This also shows a candidate's attitude towards time management.
- Communicate well with other candidates present there while waiting for an interview.
- Get more knowledge and information about the company through the material provided to candidates.

Waiting for the Interview Call

While a candidate reaches an interview destination in time, he/she may be required to sit calmly and wait for his/her turn in an adjoining room with some fellow applicants.

INSIDE THE INTERVIEW ROOM

There are certain behavioural actions whose significance cannot be underestimated when a candidate is inside the interview room. Proper attention must be paid to these small, yet very significant matters.

1. **Be Courteous** A candidate must make the most of the first few minutes of the interview as first impression is especially crucial.

   The candidate must show his full courteous side during the course of the interview. Put on a warm smile and say something courteous like, "Good morning, thank you for giving me an opportunity to be a candidate for this position."

2. **Take Your Seat** Inside the interview room if the interviewer is already seated, one must wait for a few seconds to be invited to sit down. If a candidate is not given the invitation to sit down fairly quickly, within a few seconds, ask for permission, "Excuse me, do you mind if I sit down too?' And then take your seat calmly once the permission is given. If the interviewer is standing, follow the interviewer's lead on when and where to sit down. Do not slouch, relaxing is good, slouching is bad. Sit up straight, looking professional and yet as natural as possible.
3. **Firm Handshake** A candidate must handshake with everyone using a firm but not forceful grip. Shaking hands with tips of the fingers shows lack of ability to concentrate and engage in the tasks a candidate is supposed to perform. An extremely firm handshake shows too much of aggressiveness. Good handshakes involve a firm, complete grip, eye contact and vigorous up and down movements.
4. **Maintain Calmness** It is very important to maintain one's calm and poise throughout the interview. A candidate must try to look confident and cool which indicates that he/she is not anxious or stressed about the outcome of the interview. To stay calm do some deep breathing. It can control the stress. This also conveys a candidate's willingness to answer the questions in a positive tone, not with fumbling or with forced coercion.
5. **Control on Voice** Speaking in a clear and controlled voice conveys confidence. One must avoid speaking in a monotonous tone by varying tone and pitch. Sudden change or too much unexpected or surprising change in how loud one is can lead to a sense that the candidate is just not stable and may not be suitable for a job that requires responsibility. Voice shaking should be avoided. Try to use one's own voice rather than putting on a formal public speaking voice.
6. **Quick and Smart while Answering** The interviewer asks many questions from the prospective candidate. One must remember that his/her answers must be balanced and intelligent but he/she should be quick with his/her reply. If you simply cannot come up with a response to a question, take a moment to think but do not take too long. If you get really stuck, ask the interviewer if you can come back to that question. Such a request is a risky strategy that may eliminate a candidate, but it's better than not answering at all.

7. **Positive Attitude** A candidate has to make an extra effort to show positive attitudes and do not give any negative vibes. Talk about what you can do, not what you can't. If anyone can believe in himself/herself and show the interviewer that whatever the problem you could solve it eventually, will certainly place that person high in the eyes of the interviewer.

   It can be believed through positive attitude that a person is going to be an asset to the organisation.

8. **Control Over Facial Expression** Facial expressions are powerful communicators. During the course of an interview it is very important to control one's facial expressions specially if interview is not going on your unexpected lines. It is very difficult to control expressions very often our faces communicate our deepest feelings, which one may not want to reveal. If we are not able to control our facial expressions, our credibility can be undermined and interview can go wrong or the candidate may be eliminated.

9. **Present Yourself as Confident and Ambitious** Lack of confidence and ambition can send wrong signals to the interviewer. Ambition and confidence are two of the great drivers of career and success. Confidence can often trump competence and ambition can often get any one ahead where ability doesn't. This fact is known to the interviewer and he/she would certainly prefer a candidate who is confident and ambitious.

10. **Proper Eye Contact** Proper eye contact is essential in an interview. It shows that he/she is a good listener. The candidate, during the interview need to instigate direct eye-contact and maintain it. But one must avoid appearing as if one is staring aggressively by blinking at regular intervals and nodding head every now and then.
    Looking downwards constantly makes one appear insincere or submissive. In panel interviews, it is best to look at and direct answer to the person asking the question with a periodic glance at the other members.

11. **Be a Good Listener** Generally during an interview, job candidates are primarily focussed on providing correct answers to interview questions. But listening is just as important as answering questions. Only when a candidates listens properly, then only, he is able to give the best responses. Effective listening enables job seekers to build rapport with the interviewer because the interaction is more give and take rather than giving canned answers.
12. **Answer the Questions Honestly and Thoughtfully** A candidate must never lie about his achievements, interests or skills. Lying about one's work or strengths would only cause distress in future. Even when a person does not have the required work experience, work habits of the past jobs or interest and basic skills can tell a lot about a candidate's possibility for future success. When talking about past employment, make sure that he/she speaks in a positive yet honest manner. Also refrain from speaking or making any personal comments about co-workers or employers.
13. **Avoid Sounding Desperate About Job** During the interview some candidates do not pay attention to what they say or about their body language. Sometimes an answer given by the candidate may reflect his desperation about the job so one has to be very careful while answering the questions. Do not ever try to show impatience or impolite behavior.

AFTER THE INTERVIEW

1. **Leave the Chair Only When Interviewer Asks** The candidate should never be in a hurry to leave the chair or the room after the interview is over. Wait for the nod from the chairman. Leave the room only when one is asked to. Patience is the key word during a job interview.
2. **Don't Be in a Hurry to Leave** Some candidates are so nervous that they feel like running away from the place as soon as the interview is over. It should not be so. You must leave the room only when you are permitted to leave. Never show your eagerness to leave the room or place it may signal wrong indications.
3. **Grab the Opportunity of Hand Shake, If Given** The candidate should not be over-enthusiastic after the interview is over and offer his/her hand first for handshake. But if he/she gets an opportunity to handshake with the interviewer, he must grab the opportunity and shake hands. Your way of hand shaking offers an opportunity to the interviewer to decide in favour or against the selection of a candidate.
4. **While Leaving Put the Chair Properly** Don't make any noise while leaving. After a candidate gets up to leave, he/she must remember to place the chair at the correct position Manners are being watched at every step. After the interviewer asks the candidate to leave and he/she started to walk back to the door, don't look back. The candidate is being observed with regard to his/her manner of leaving the room.
5. **Thank All Interviewers Inside the Room** There may be more than one interviewer inside the interview room. A candidate must thank each and every person inside the interview room as he/she is about to leave. One must leave the job interview leaving behind a positive impression. A small sentence like "It was nice meeting you all and learning about the organisation was a great experience", can do wonders in leaving a positive impression about a candidate.

DON'TS INSIDE THE INTERVIEW ROOM

What a candidate should not do inside the interview room is almost as important as what he should do. This section deals with some issues/matters which should not be carried out inside interview room.

1. **Don't Forget to Take Permission to Come Inside** It is common courtesy to take permission to enter inside the interview room. The candidate must not forget to take the interviewer's permission to come inside the room.
2. **Don't Change Sitting Postures** During an interview, the sitting posture taken by a candidate should not convey any casualness on the part of the candidate. You may adopt any sitting posture you are comfortable with. However the candidate has to ensure that he/she conveys seriousness. Postures should be classic 'sit straight'. No leaning forward over the interviewer's desk.
3. **Don't Start Any Debate While Answering** Basic courtesy requires a candidate to be restrained in his response. Do not start any unruly debate. One has to be very measured in one's responses during an interview. Try to encourage answers that provides insight into personalities, leadership skills and integrity.
4. **Don't Ignore Cross Questions** There may be times when two or three members shoot questions at the candidate in a row. Don't get disturbed but do not ignore any questions try to answer them one by one. Make a polite comment that you would answer all the questions not together but one by one.
5. **Don't Criticise Previous Employer** Do not say negative things about your previous employer, boss or colleagues. Even if some one's boss was not good or reasonable never state real feeling to a probable boss. Most of the interviewer will cut the person's name from the list if he/she goes about criticising the previous employer. No matter how reasonable one's complaint may be but if disrespect is shown to the previous boss, the chances of any one getting a job diminish fast as it will be assumed that one would be disrespectful to the probable boss also.

6. **Don't Ask Question About Salary** Even though salary may be of utmost importance to most of the candidates, do not harp on it all time along as it can certainly put off any interviewer. During the first interview, the candidate should not, as a rule, ask about salary, benefits or holidays. If a candidate is asked about his/her salary expectations too early in the process of an interview, an ideal reply would be that he/she would rather postpone that discussion until you had more information about his/her duties and responsibilities.
7. **Don't Try to Change the Topic Until it is Changed by the Interviewer** A candidate sometimes tries to change the topic during a job interview as he may not be very well versed in that particular one. Never make this mistake. If one tries to change the topic it may indicate a candidate's non-professional and unintelligent action. This may also indicate one's unpreparedness for the interview.
8. **Don't Indulge in Political Controversy** A candidate must remember not to act in an immature way by raking up politically controversial issues. A candidate must show how balanced he is by not indulging in any cultural, religious or political conversation. One should not try to gain the favour of the interviewer by taking a stand against or in favour of any particular community.
9. **Don't Miss the Opportunity to Thank the Interview on Praising You** Sometimes an interviewer praises a candidate for smart dress or other achievement. The candidate should be prompt enough to take this praise in a positive manner and thank the interviewer immediately. Basic courtesies should never be forgotten.

The Interview Process

In Interview process certain steps have to be followed one by one to judge a candidate's behaviour and knowledge and decide his suitability for a given job. An interview follows various steps to reach the conclusion.

Step I : Initiating the Interview

↓

Step II : Exposing the Candidate's Academic Level

↓

Step III : Analysis of Candidate's Behavioural and Interpersonal Qualities

↓

Step IV : Summing UP

↓

Step V : Arriving at a Conclusion

Process of Interview

STEP I : INITIATING THE INTERVIEW

In this stage, discussion commences informally with the candidate by being asked a few encouraging questions to make him/her feel at ease. The most popular methods to initiate an interview are

i. Initiation based on Candidate's Biodata/Family Background

Before interviewee enters in the interview hall, members of the interview board have candidate's resume, portfolio and other material regarding his/her background, education, special skills and interests.

Interviewer should be friendly and should smile and greet candidate by his/her name. This will warm-up the candidate and prepared him/her to face any challenge. e.g.

"Come in Mr. Bharadwaz"

or "Mrs Geetika, you are welcome"

or "Mr Ranade, please come in and take your seat."

Such an initiation helps in building a cordial atmosphere where interview can begin. To put the candidate at ease some low key questions are asked. These questions help to establish a rapport with the candidate as well as put him at ease so that he may answer the question without being nervous or stressed.

Every candidate must pay attention to his/her name or surname as every name conveys a meaning and the candidate must be aware of any significance or literary meaning of his/her own name.

EXAMPLE

(Example showing an interview initiated on the basis of biodata)

Chairman So you are Mr. Gaurav Nath. That's a nice name.

Gaurav Thank you Sir.

Chairman Can you tell us what does your name denote?

Gaurav Sir it means pride or honour.

Chairman O.K. Gaurav, that's fine.

Other questions usually asked to initiate the interview can be on his/her educational background or about the college/university from where the candidate has done graduation or post graduation. Some other questions based on a candidate's bio-data can be

"So Mr Sameer you have done masters from Pune University but did your graduation from Mumbai University. Which university has a better standard of education and offers more opportunities according to you?

Or

Mrs Suman, you have secured high marks in English Literature. Is this the most interesting subject for you?

Or

Mr Singh, you are from Meerut University. Generally this university is in lime light due to all wrong reasons. Is it correct?

Based on such preliminary question the interviewer would like to create a comfort zone for the candidate. These questions also lead to further lines of inquiry by the interviewer. The candidate must answer these questions carefully.

ii. Initiation Based on Candidate's Interests and Hobbies

Before asking questions related to the main field or to make the candidate feel at ease questions regarding a candidates' interest and hobbies are also asked by interviewer.

For example Mrs Jyoti you have mentioned reading as your hobby. Tell me which is the latest book you have read and what did you like about it?

A candidate must remember that interviewer does not want to trap anyone but of course a candidate's verbal articulation, vocabulary and genuineness about interests and hobbies are certainly watched especially any variance, positive or negative, from the standard.

Every person has a certain past time hobby and interest. While answering question on the hobby one should be honest and straight forward and should not mention exotic or unusual hobbies for the sake of making a great impression. Many candidates tell lies about their hobbies so as to impress the interviewer. This is not correct practise as there are chances to be caught in one's own web of lies. Certain hobbies generally mentioned by the candidates are—reading news paper, novels or books, listening to good music, cooking, gardening, watching movies. Candidate should be frank and prepare answers related to different hobbies beforehand.

EXAMPLE

(Example showing an interview initiated on the basis of interests and Hobbies)

Chairman Miss Bajaj, you have mentioned in your biodata that your hobby is visiting new places in your own country.

Ankita Bajaj Sir, India is full of marvellous places. I like to visit one of the unexplored areas each time I plan a visit. There is so much to see, to learn and to imbibe from our own culture. Different places replicate different culture and I get mesmerised by it.

Chairman Which place did you visit last before attending this interview?

Ankita	Sir, my last visit was to a place called Dharmkot in Distt. Kangra, Himachal Pradesh. It is situated on the crest of hill, 11 km from Dharamshala and 2 kms, from Mcleodganj. The place spots a panoramic view of Kangra valley and Dhauladhar ranges. It is a good base for trekkers also.
Chairman	Ankita, visiting new places costs money also. How do you afford travelling?
Ankita	Sir, I do not waste money on watching movies or eating out very frequently. I try to save it to meet expenses of travelling.
Member	OK Miss Ankita, that's fine.

iii. Initiation Based on General Awareness

General awareness is a vast, endless area and questions asked can be tricky or difficult. Questions may be asked on current national or international matters, political situation in the country, controversies raging among nations or confrontation of ideologies.

A candidate must come prepared reading books of general knowledge, newspapers, magazines and various articles discussed at the social media. It is possible that a candidate may be able to impress the interviewer at the rapport building level, but his/her real test starts from now.

The question in this step will usually be probing or leading questions testing your awareness, quickness in replying and your outlook on different matters. Sometimes interviewer may asks interviewee's opinion about any current political situation or about solution of certain problem related to state or nation, one should reply firmly and fearlessly. Certain question can be asked to test your general knowledge such as

- Do you know what is current burning issue in India?
- What would you do to eradicate corruption in your country?

These questions are asked just to prove that you are interested in current affairs and should be prepared for such questions.

iv. Initiation through Odd Questions

Sometime, interviewer asks some confusing question or odd question which might confuse you but they are meant to assess your behaviour in a tricky situation. *Some confusing questions may be as follows* :

- How did you reach this place?
- How did you reach this floor? By the lift or staircase?

For answering such type of questions, you have to be alert and pay attention to details so that you are able to give spontaneous response.

Example regarding first question

If you say by taxi or by autorickshaw they may ask autorickshaw number or taxi number etc.

STEP II : EXPOSING THE CANDIDATE'S ACADEMIC LEVEL

This is the difficult and crucial part of the interview. The answer should match with your knowledge and academic level as elaborated in resume. Your basics should be clear and must be supported by examples. A student of economics, for e.g. may be asked to, "could you explain what economics is all about?"

After brief introductory exchange the conversation and the questions asked become narrower and more focussed. If there is a job interview, the interviewer tries to find out a candidate's suitability for the post through a variety of questions related to his field of study and the job experience.

For the admission in research institute or any other interview organised by government or private institution or organisation, questions asked will seek information on a candidate's academic knowledge and its application in present day situation. The main subject can be one in which a candidate may have obtained a master's degree or may have done specialisation.

To tackle such questions, a candidate is required to know the correlation between that subject, its practical applicability and its usefulness to the job for which he/she is being interviewed.

EXAMPLE

(Example showing the candidates academic level)

Chairman How will your knowledge of English Literature will help in adminstrative work?

Anuj Sayal Sir Literature unlocks the culture of time period and it allows us to interpret our own life and emotions. It teaches us to connect to other human beings.

Chairman You are just giving me the meaning of Literature. Can you explain me how this will help in adminstration?

Anuj Sayal Sir, Literature give us an insight-into the human mind and emotion. To be a good administrature one must be able to understand the people who are working with you or the people you have to deal with. A widely read person will certainly be able to relate to any problem easily.

STEP III : ANALYSIS OF CANDIDATE'S INTERPERSONAL QUALITIES

A candidate's personality traits and interpersonal skills play a vital role in deciding his/her suitability for the job. After testing academic skills of a candidate, a series of questions are asked to assess about a candidate's potential and abilities. Employers seek a person having strong interpersonal skills, who can work well in team and be able to communicate effectively with co-workers, customers and clients. People with good interpersonal skills are usually perceived as optimistic, calm, confident and charismatic qualities. Candidate should have some behavioural characteristics such as adaptable, articulate, accountable, listener, focused, confident, enthusiastic, high integrity, self directed, effective networker.

If a candidate is looking for a change in job, particularly a change in career he/she must learn to appreciate the flexibility of his/her skills, knowledge and experience. It is best to be specific as far as possible.

Some questions to explore behavioural and interpersonal skills are

- Describe the work environment or culture in which you have experienced the most success.
- Describe three components of your philosophy of management that demonstrate what you value and add as an individual, to an organisation's culture and work environment.

STEP IV : SUMMING UP

This is the is the final step in the process of interview. The candidate must have firm views on what he /she has stated earlier. There are chances that the interviewer may ask the same question in a different manner. A candidate is likely to be rejected if his/her views are not consistent on an issue. Before interview is about to close the chairman may invite other board members to pose any questions to the candidate one must be fully energetic and confident even if it is the fag end of interview. Attend all other members with equal interest and answer with confidence.

A candidate should remain seated even when no members of the interview board have any questions to ask. He/She should leave the room when the chairman asks him clearly to leave. Maintain the basic courtesies and do not forget to thank all the members including the chairman while leaving, rise up quietly and leave the room without making any noise and close the door quietly while going out of the interview room.

EXAMPLE

(Example showing how to conclude or sum up the interview)

Chairman Miss Gunjan Saini, do you have any question to ask us?

Gunjan No, Sir, thank you very much.

Chairman (Addresses the member of the interview board and says) Is there anything else you would like to discuss with 'Miss Saini?

Member No, that's enough we think. (Candidate keeps sitting without giving any indication that she is either in a hurry or in a state of tension and wants to leave the room as early as possible)

Chairman All right, Miss Saini, that-will be all. You may go now, please.

Gunjan (Takes her paper and file and get up) Thank you, Sir.

Many candidates concentrate all energies on how to answer the interview question while preparing for an interview. But one must remember that interview provides an opportunity to the candidate also to evaluate whether the particular job suits him or is good for him/her.

When given a chance, the candidate must use the platform to ask valid questions and gather information about the company, industry and job profile. This will also signal the interviewer that the candidate is interested in the job and is aware of current industry situation.

Some questions are given below for a candidate, that he or she can ask during interview

- What are day to day expectations and responsibilities of this job?
- Can you describe the company's management style?
- Does the organisation support ongoing training and education for employees to stay updated in their fields?
- Are lateral or rotational job moves available?
- What is the organisation's policy on transfers to other divisions or other offices?
- What would my initial assignments be?
- What type of appraisal system do you have?
- What are the career growth opportunities in this organisation?
- What are the traits and skills of people who are the most successful within the organisation?

STEP V : ARRIVING AT A CONCLUSION

Every step of interview is important and has to be taken care of. One should try to close the interview by telling the interviewers that he/she is interested in that particular job.

The closing is generally mixed up with the feedback and a candidate may get this statement, "Thanks for coming, I'm going to review your file and we'll get in touch with you after sometime later."

In this stage, interview board assigns marks against each of the following personality traits.

- Overall performances
- Academic level
- Self confidence
- Communication skills
- Overall behaviour etc.

Each member make his/her own comments and submits the result of candidate to the concerned authority.

REASONS WHY PEOPLE DONT'S GET HIRED

Reaching Late A candidate should neither reach very late nor very early for the interview. Reaching 15 minutes before his scheduled time is ideal.

Lack of Basic Courtesy Do not pester or be rude to the receptionist or other staff. The interviewers very often solicit a receptionist's opinion of candidate.

Poor Attire A candidate's dress must be appropriate for the organisation, the position and the nature of the job. A poorly dressed person does not give a good first impression, shows sloppiness.

Errors in HR Form Filling Every information is cross checked so there should be no error while filling up the HR form.

Lack of Organisational Knowledge Knowledge about the organisation shows a candidate's initiative and interest in the job.

Looking Anxious/ Nervous Lack of confidence leads to nervousness and undue anxiety may lead to fumbling and inability to express clearly.

Laughing and Speaking Loudely Appropriate behaviour is expected at the time of interview as it is a formal event and modesty should be maintained at all levels.

Criticising Previous Employer Criticising previous employer shows that you have a negative attitude.

Taking Phone Call in the Middle of the Interview Not acceptable norm, generally mobile should be switched off during the interview as it creates diversion and reflects your disinterest.

Asking Illogical Question Asking questions about salary, promotion, work from home facility should be avoided as it reflects that you are not interested in learning.

Post Interview Activity

After the interview is over, after all hard work and answering all difficult questions, there are certain things which are still left to be done as the magic words "when can you start" are still deluding the prospective candidate. There are certain steps which should be followed after the interview is over.

Collect All Contact Information

Before leaving the interview venue, one must lay the ground work for effective follow up. The candidate may ask for business cards of the chairman or other members who have interviewed him/her or he can write down the names and contact information for each person.

Conduct a Self-Evaluation

After the interview is over, conduct a self-evaluation of where you performed well and where you went wrong. If you found yourself uncomfortable answering the particular question or you were not able to give appropriate answer. Be prepared for next time. This type of self-evaluation will be beneficial to the candidate for future performance. This self evaluation can be used to polish and perfect the next performance if it is required.

Reach out to References

A candidate must contact his references immediately after a job interview. If he has done well in the interview the chances are that the references will be contacted for confirmation about the qualities, achievements of a candidate. A timely alert to the references can always be useful and beneficial.

Follow Up With HR Department

Follow up with HR Department is very essential whether or not a candidate is truly in the running. Sometimes the interviewer can get crazy busy and it is important to always follow up with a note and even a call in a week if there is no word back on next steps.

Candidates should never be afraid to ask for acknowledgement and closure, even if it's not the news they want to hear. The follow up is a way to reiterate a candidate's interest and reaffirm why the candidate is the best fit for the role. It may not be able to turn around an interview that did not go well, but it could be something that could help differentiate a candidate from equally strong candidates.

Send a Thank Note

A follow up Thank You letter to the interviewer is an important step in the interviewing process. A lot of job seekers often forget or think a letter of thank you, a waste of time. But we must remember that sending such a letter is not only proper business etiquette but it also makes a candidate stand out from other candidates competing for the same position.

Many a time, this thank you note to the prospective employer may prove to be a clincher; it serves as a reminder of a candidate's qualities and the initial impression the interviewer had formed of a candidate.

One should be alert enough to remember the name of the person who conducted the interview and his correct title and your letter must be addressed to him only.

Sample Letter (Thank You Note)

Mandeep Malhotra
Jaishree Dhan Society
Andheri West
Mumbai, (Maharashtra)

10th July, 2016

Mr BL Naidu
Chief Manager, (HR)
Business News Delhi
New Delhi

Dear Mr Naidu,

Thank you for taking out time to interview me yesterday for the position of Chief Editor with 'Business News Daily'.

It was a pleasure meeting you. I truly enjoyed learning more about the role and the company. After our conversation. I am confident that my skills and experiences are a great match for this opportunity.

I would greatly appreciate a follow up as you move forward with the hiring process. Thanks again and I hope to hear from you in the near future. If you need any additional information from me, please let me know.

Best regards
Mandeep Malhotra

Letter of Acceptance

If a candidate is selected and invited to join the organisation, a short letter is required to be sent to his/her prospective employer. The letter should be written immediately after receiving the phone call about your selection.

Sample Letter (Acceptance)

The Chief Manager (HR)
27, Metclif House
New Delhi

18th June, 2016

Dear Sir,

It was certainly a wonderful news when I received a phone call this afternoon offering me a position of Senior Manager (Operation) in your esteemed organisation. As desired I will join the company with immediate effect and report to Miss Neeti Nair in the personnel department on Monday, 20th June at 9 : 00 AM sharp.

Thank you again for offering me this wonderful opportunity. Please let me know if I can do anything in advance of my start date to facilitate the paper work.

Best regards
Yours truly
Roopali Aggarwal

Sample of Job Rejection Letter

(Turning down a Job Offer)

Regardless of the reason a candidate is not accepting a job offer, writing a job rejection letter is the right thing to do. It is professional etiquette to write a letter to the HR department or hiring authority. The purpose of this letter is to notify an employer of your decision. Such letter should be brief and courteous. In the same way, a company must send a rejection letter stating some decent reason that particular candidate was not hired because of it. We will study two types of rejection letters.

Sample Letter (Rejected by the Candidate)

25th June, 2016

Mr Purushottam Kashyap
HR Manager,
Greenley Corp. Inc.
Jalvayu Towers, Gurgaon

Dear Mr Purushottam,

Thank you for offering me the manager position (HR) in your company. However, I am unable to accept your offer as it has come a little late and I have already accepted job in another company.

I am pleased that your company considered me for this position. Thank you once again for the interview and your precious time spent with me. It was a pleasure meeting you and learning about Greenley Corp. Inc.

Best regards
Yours Truly
Tanu Anand

Sample Letter (Rejected by the Employer)

Clear Line Systems
155, Signature Towers,
Gurgaon, Haryana

26th June, 2016

Dear Rohit Nair,

Thank you for taking the time to meet with our team about the position of a System Analyst in Clear Line Systems. It was a pleasure to interact with you and to know more about your skills.

Unfortunately, our team did not select you for further consideration.

I would like to note that competition for jobs here is always strong and that we often have to make difficult choices between many high-calibre candidates. We will be keeping your resume on file for future openings that better fits your profile.

We will be happy to send feedback if you want any.

Thanks again and best of luck with your job search.

Regards
Mani Ratnam
(Hiring Manager)

CONTINUE WITH JOB-SEARCHING AT OTHER PLACES

Sometimes getting an appropriate job becomes really difficult. One rejection after another can really demotivate a person. Some tips should be kept in mind of dealing with a job rejection. Do not use a job interview as a measure of professional worth. One should not pin all hopes on one specific job in the belief that it is perfect.

One must pursue multiple opportunities even when one is not in its need. If a candidate has faced job rejection at many places, he must try to get feed back from the employer as constructive feed back will certainly help a candidate to boost up his confidence.

One should try to focus on his strengths and identify opportunities that one is passionate about. The best way to deal with rejection is to keep a smile on one's face. One should learn to turn each rejection into a learning opportunity and stay focused on one's ultimate goal.

SAMPLE INTERVIEWS FOR GOVERNMENT SECTOR

- *For Civil Services*
- *For Defence Services*
- *For Banking/Railway Sector*
- *For Intelligence Bureau/LIC*
- *For Other Examinations*

Sample interviews provide encounter with real time questions to the interviewee. Here we are providing some mock interviews for the government sector specially designed with most probable questions asked in such interviews.

1. SAMPLE INTERVIEW FOR CIVIL SERVICES EXAMINATION (IAS)

Deepankar Saberwal is a smart young man from Punjab. He is MBBS from Medical College, Meerut. He is fair complexioned with above average height and lean athletic built. He is wearing a cream coloured shirt and dark brown trouser with a matching tie and light brown shoes.

He examines the seating plan and confirms the time of his interview. Thereafter he moves over to the waiting room where he can sit, study and relax till his turn for the interview. Soon his name is announced, whereupon, he confidently proceeds to the interview room with firm and steady steps. Before going in, he gently taps on the door to obtain formal permission.

Deepankar May I come in, Sirs.

Chairman Yes Mr. Deepankar, please come and take your seat.

Deepankar (Enters the room and says) Thank you Sir and Good morning to you all, Sirs.

NOTE *(He sits down smartly in the chair and awaits the next observation or move from the Board).*

Chairman Mr. Deepankar we note that you have done MBBS. How do you think that with the degree of a doctor you can become a good administrator?

Deepankar Sir, during our study at the Medical College, we got enough opportunity to have close contact with patients, to listen and sense their problems, to analyse their behavioural attitude and also the areas which need to be focused upon to provide good health conditions.

During my training as a doctor, I realised the fact that the cleanliness and the general hygenic conditions of a place are the true indicators of the actual state of the society. A clean city with good hygienic conditions leaves a better impression than a dirty one does.

With such experience and knowledge coupled with administrative power, I felt I could contribute a great deal in providing good health conditions.

Member 2 You have been trained for being a successful doctor. How can you expect to succeed as an administrator like a district collector or divisional commissioner?

Deepankar Just like we have to undergo internship for one year after completing the MBBS degree to actually qualify as a doctor, IAS officers also go through the same process. The focus of the training programme at Lal Bahadur Shastri National Academy of Administration (LBSNAA), is to equip the IAS officers for the first 10 years of service, during which they are also expected to serve as District Magistrates (DM). First the foundation course of 15 weeks duration imparts an understanding of the machinery of the government and of the political, social, economic and administrative environment. The Foundation Course also fosters greater coordination among different civil services.

This is followed by the 26 week long IAS Professional Course (Phase I) which covers the topics of Governance, Ethics and Leadership, Public Administration and Management, Law, State and Local Public Finance, Human and Social Development and District and Regulatory Administration. Thus, it gives the necessary theoretical training, just like doctors are given during MBBS. After that the trainees work in the field for one year, just like we have internship for doctors. The officers then go back to LBSNAA for Phase II of the course which covers Public Administration, Management, Law, Economics, Computers and Language.

This means that a candidate from any field can succeed as an IAS officer because he has been given adequate grounding in all related subjects besides getting practical experience in the field for one year. So I am confident that I can succeed as an administrator.

Member 1 Can you outline the broad difference between the Homeopathic and Allopathic system of treatment?

Deepankar Allopathy is the western system of medicine. 'Allo' has been derived from the Greek word Allos which means other. Allopathy, therefore, implies the treatment of a disease by other drugs, i.e. drugs having effects opposite to the symptoms. So, we can say that allopathy is based on the principle 'opposite cures opposite'.

On the other hand, homeopathy is the system of treating diseases by administering minute quantities of drugs which would if given in larger doses to a healthy person produce symptoms similar to those of the disease. The word 'homeo' has been derived from the Greek words Homos meaning 'same' and Pathos meaning 'morbid condition'. In other words, homeopathy is based on the principle 'like cures like'.

Member 1 Mr. Deepankar what is complementary and alternate medicines or therapy? Why are many people in the world using these medicines for treatment of various diseases?

Deepankar Sir complementary medicine is a group of diagnostic and therapeutic disciplines that are used together with conventional medicine. Alternative medicine is the term for medical products and practices that are not part of standard care and are used in place of standard medical care. Examples of alternative practices include homeopathy, acupuncture, traditional medicines, aromatherapy, meditation, yoga, etc. A new government report in USA shows that Americans spend a good chunk of their health care dollars on alternative medicines as they believe enough in the value of these approaches. But people trying complementary or alternative medicines for a particular problem must discuss it with their doctor.

Member 2 Mr. Deepankar you belong to Punjab. What is the state of economy in your home state, Punjab?

Deepankar Sir, Punjab state has an agrarian economy as this region is an ideal place for growth of wheat, rice, fruits, sugarcane and various vegetables. Punjab is described as 'India's bread basket' or 'Granary of India'. 19.5% of total wheat and 11% of total rice in India, are grown in this state. As against an all India average of 51% it has 85% of its area under cultivation. The manufacturing sector is expanding since late 20th century. The industries with huge number of workers include silk, textile and wood industry along with beverages and processed food, leather goods, hosiery and rubber and plastics. Punjab produces about 70% of best cotton quality in the country. Some other sectors which have given a boost to the economy of Punjab are dairy industry, sugar and transportation, banking and finance.

Member 3 Mr. Deepankar what do we mean by the term 'Medical Tourism'?

Deepankar Yes Sir, Medical Tourism refers to the travel made by people to another country for the purpose of obtaining medical treatment in that country.

Chairman What are the advantages of medical treatment in India for the foreigners?

Deepankar Some of the advantages of medical treatment in India to the people of other countries are the reduced cost, the availability of latest medical technologies, a growing compliance on international quality standards. Most estimates found that treatment costs in India start at around one-tenth of the price of comparable treatment in the United States or the United Kingdom.

Member The Central Institute of Medical and Aromatic Plants, a research institute of CSIR Lucknow has published some papers on wonder plant 'Basil?' Why is this report important?

Deepankar The papers or report published by CSIR is about the whole genome sequence of the wonder plant 'Holy Basil or Tulsi. The availability of the whole genome sequence will help to provide scientific validity to the traditional claims of this herb's utility in diverse medicinal usage.

Member 1 What is the contribution of Yoga in improving the quality of life of an individual?

Deepankar Man is a physical, mental and spiritual being and Yoga helps to promote a balanced development of all the three. At the physical level, the methods comprise various yoga postures or *asanas* that aim to keep the body healthy. The mental techniques include breathing exercises or *pranayama* and meditation or *dhyana* to discipline the mind. The ultimate goal of Yoga is to transcend the self and attain enlightenment. As the Bhagavad-Gita says, "A person is said to have achieved yoga, the union with the self, when the perfectly disciplined mind gets freedom from all desires and becomes absorbed in the self alone". Thus, Yoga improves the overall quality of life of the person practising it regularly. In contrast, other forms of physical exercises like aerobics assure only physical well-being. They have little to do with the development of the spiritual or astral body.

Chairman Do you favour the creation of an All-India Judicial Service on the lines of the IAS and IPS?

Rajvanshi Sir, the idea of having an All-India Judicial Service has been in circulation for over two decades now. The Law Commission has favoured in and the 42nd Amendment of the Constitution provides for the creation of Indian Judicial Service to cover all judicial officers for the rank of additional district judge and above.

However, the recommendation has not so far been implemented as the states, in general, are opposed to it. They feel that the creation of such a service would curtail the state autonomy. Even state High Courts are opposing the creation of an All-India Judicial Service since, it would mean losing their hold on the subordinate courts under them in the State. But, I feel, for the purpose of national integration and having a merit-based cadre, an All-India Judicial Service should come into being immediately. In fact, we should also have an All-India Educational Service on such lines. To be frank, I am in favour of anything that will promote national integration and would simultaneously give weightage to merit and performance.

Member 3 What does it imply when we say India is a secular state?

Deepankar It implies that India is a state where multiple religions like Hinduism, Christianity, Muslim, Sikh, etc exist in our country, which makes it secular. All citizens following different religions are treated equally and religion of any one cannot be imposed on the other when it comes to his/her Fundamental Rights.

Member 2 It is said that the word 'secular' is a dubious word, capable of diverse meanings. Has this not caused confusion and has been misused by the interested parties?

Deepankar The word 'secular' has many meanings and has caused confusion among the teachers of political science and law. But this state of confusion has been set at rest by authoritative pronouncements made by the Supreme Court.

These are, (i) Secularism in India does not mean that the state should be hostile to religion but that it should be neutral as between the different religions.

(ii) Every individual has the freedom to profess and practice his own religion and it cannot be contended that 'if a person is a devout Hindu or a devout Muslim, he ceases to be secular.'

(iii) The neutrality of the state would be violated if religion is used for political purposes and advocated by the political parties for their political ends. It is in this sense that secularism is to be regarded as basic feature of the Constitution.

Member 3 Don't you think Mr. Deepankar that the strained relations between India and Pakistan will come in the way of establishing cordial relations with the Islamic countries of West Asia and South-East Asia.

Deepankar India, has the second largest Muslim population in the world. If Indian Muslims live in peace, prosperity and contentment, all the Islamic world will ignore Pakistan's propaganda. So as long as India stays by its secular ideals, it will be able to maintain cordial relationship with all nations of the world irrespective of their religious moorings.

Member 4 What is GST bill and how it is going to boost Indian economy?

Deepankar The Goods and Service Tax (GST) is a Value Added Tax that will replace all indirect taxes levied on goods and services by the Indian Central and State Governments once it is implemented.

The GST is all set to consolidate all state economies. This will be one of the biggest taxation reforms that will take place in India once the bill gets passed. GST will not be a cost to registered retailers therefore there will be no hidden taxes and the cost of doing business will be lower. This in turn will help export being more competitive.

Chairman Mr. Deepankar what is dual control in context of GST bill?

Deepankar Sir, dual control means control of both the centre as well as states as far as GST collection is concerned. Dual control would mean a businessman will have to file the details of sales transactions with both the central and state and may also have to take necessary licence from both for the purpose of GST. Small businesses may find it very difficult to deal with two agencies for a single purpose of GST.

Member 1 Mr. Deepankar, what is Missile Technology Control Regime? Why its membership is a big boost for India?

Deepankar The Missile Technology Control Regime (MTCR) is a multilateral export control regime. It is an informal and voluntary partnership among 35 countries to prevent the proliferation of missile and unmanned aerial vehicle technology capable of carrying above 500 kg payload for more than 300 km.

India is the 35th country to join its membership. This membership is expected to facilitate high technology tie ups with Indian industry and ease access to high-tech items for space and defence programmes. The membership will enable India to buy high-end missiles technology as well as increase its joint venture with Russia. India's entry into MTCR also implies that it will find it easier to export missiles like BrahMos.

Member 1 Why are some corruption scandals named Barkhagate, Radiagate, CWGgate etc?

Deepankar The names are inspired from the Watergate scandal of USA in the 1970s when the 1972 Presidential Election was held there. The Watergate scandal resulted due to a break-in inside the Democratic National Committee headquarters at the Watergate office complex in Washington, DC. The effects of the scandal ultimately led to the resignation of US President. It also resulted in the indictment, trial, conviction and incarceration of several Nixon administration officials. The Republicans had installed a recording system in the Democratic Party office by breaking into it and recorded many campaign conversations of their rivals with the approval of President Nixon.

Member 2 Has UNO been able to solve the problem of terrorism around the world?

Deepankar While countering terrorism has been on the agenda of UNO for decades, the attack against the USA on 11th September, 2001 prompted the Security Council to adopt Resolution 1373 which for the first time established the Counter-Terrorism Committee (CTC). Five years later, UN Global Counter Terrorism strategy was agreed upon by all member states of the General Assembly. The strategy is a unique instrument to enhance the efforts of the international community to counter terrorism along four pillars

- Addressing conditions conducive to the spread of terrorism.
- Preventing and combating terrorism.
- Building member states capacity to prevent and combat terrorism and to strengthen the role of the United Nations system in this regard.
- Ensuring the respect for human rights for all and the rule of law as the fundamental basis for countering terrorism.

A counter terrorism implementation task-force has also been endorsed by the UN General Assembly. The United Nations Counter-Terrorism Centre (UNCCT) provides capacity building assistance to member-states and coherence within the UN system on counter-terrorism and to provide assistance to member states.

Chairman Mr. Deepankar is it relevant for the international body and developed countries to spend billions of dollars on international peace-keeping forces?

Deepankar Yes sir, UN Peacekeeping provides essential security and support to millions of people as well as fragile institutions emerging from conflict. The peacekeeper forces go to war-torn regions where no one else is willing or able to go and prevent conflicts from escalating. UN peacekeeping forces has 124000 personnel serving on 16 peace operations led by the UN department in four continents. It has impacted the lives of hundreds of millions of people.

The money spent on peacekeeping forces is worth the effort. Moreover the cost to the UN per peacekeeper has been found to be the most cost effective means of preventing a return to war in war-torn conflict prone societies.

Member OK Mr. Deepankar inspite of a busy schedule as a doctor do you pursue any hobby?

Deepankar Sir, I am fond of reading. In my spare time, I read medical journals, updating my knowledge and get acquainted with new research going on in the field of medicine.

I also like cooking as I am fond of eating tasty food; moreover it provides me with much needed relaxation.

Chairman Cooking? Wow doctor and cooking two things apart. Any way Mr. Deepankar, your interview is over. Would you like to ask any question from any of us?

Deepankar No, Sir thank you very much. I don't have any question.

Chairman You may leave now.

Deepankar Thank you Sirs. (He now gets up and leaves the room gracefully).

2. SAMPLE INTERVIEW FOR CIVIL SERVICES EXAMINATION (IAS)

Rashmi Negi is postgraduate in physics from Delhi University. She speaks with confidence, shows boldness as well as initiative and articulates herself while talking to fellow candidates in the waiting hall. She hears her name being called for the interview and proceeds towards interview room briskly but gracefully. She taps gently on the door, pauses for few seconds and then goes in after closing the door gently behind her. She walks confidently upto the seat meant for candidate.

Rashmi Good morning to all of you, Sirs.

Chairman Good Morning Miss Rashmi. Please be seated.

Rashmi Thank you Sir, (She occupies the chair meant for the candidate smartly, without unnecessary movement and noise).

Chairman Miss Rashmi, I see from your bio-data that you are a physics postgraduate who had gone in for space research. I am sure you like the research work and would like to carry on further in the same line. What has made you to give up the research and opt for the IAS?

Rashmi I was doing research in order to assist and help my former professor, since I have a lot of regard and affection for him. I am impressed with his intelligence and innovative attitude. He was in search of an associate who could assist him with his research work. After completion of my postgraduation, I offered my services for his work, which he accepted with modesty. He knew that I am preparing for IAS. That is how I got involved in research work.

Chairman As a student of Physics and Space Research what do you understand by the term NAVIC? How has India progressed in its space programmes?

Rashmi India's own navigation system, the set up for which was completed on 28th April, 2016 with the launch of the seventh and final satellite is called NAVIC (Navigation with Indian Constellation).

The Indian space programme has soared height since last decades as a result of drastic improvement in the technology. The seventh and final satellite of the Indian Regional Navigation Satellite System IRNSS-1G was launched on board the PSLV (Polar Satellite Launch Vehicle) on 28th April only.

Now ISRO can focus on the progress of designing front end chips which will receive the navigational signals sent out by the satellites. These satellites launched by the government have made the people's life easier. We can now be proud of this achievement in space programme.

It was a record for India as it was the maximum number of satellites India has put in space at one go.

Member 1 As India successfully launched 20 satellites in a single mission on 22nd June, 2016. Out of these satellites, how many are commercial satellites and of which country? What is India's main cargo in this launch? How is it going to be useful for India?

Rashmi There were 17 commercial satellites of which belonged to USA. India's main cargo is 725.5 kg Cartosat-2 series satellite for Earth observation. The images sent by Cartosat will be useful for cartographic, urban, rural, coastal land use, water distribution and other applications.

Member 3 Miss Rashmi, could you explain why there are so many political parties and splinter groups in Kerala and why it has been unable to have a single party government, with adequate legislative majority till 2016?

Rashmi Kerala, as you know, is one of the smaller states in India with very limited land area. Even within the area of its borders, we have substantial mountainous terrain. On the sea-coast we have plenty of back-bay terrain. Despite population control, the density of population in Kerala per square kilometre is quite high.

Next, there are sizeable numbers, with concentration in specific areas, of different religious groups like Hindus, Muslims and Christians. The Hindus are further divided into two large groups of forward communities and backward communities. Thirdly, the percentage of literacy in Kerala is the highest in India.

Educated people, unlike illiterate ones, have their independent political views on various issues and cannot be easily misled by consideration of caste, creed, language, religion, etc.

They would therefore, join a political outfit nearly conforming to their political convictions. There is not enough job or land to go around. There is thus acute unemployment and poverty. Hence, the unscrupulous political leaders can play upon the regional, communal and economic susceptibilities of the people. Since the population is equally divided with concentrated pockets of communities, it is difficult for any party to get absolute majority.

Because of multiplicity of parties, Kerala had suffered instablity in the past but now a coalition era has set in. It is either communist led Left Democractic Front (LDF) or Congress led United Democratic Front (UDF) which rules the state alternately. It is the turn of LDF this time which has won 91 seats in recent elections.

Member 1 What is your recommended solution to the situation as outlined by you in Kerala?

Rashmi Sir, the division of the states on the linguistic basis is the greatest blunder we have made. The right thing would be to have state boundaries in terms of self-sufficiency in resources. There should be some correlation between population, area, natural resources like water, land, minerals, rivers, sea coast, communication facilities and some natural and historical boundaries.

Multi-lingual states will promote national unity. There will be an end to the linguistic quarrels and sons-of-soil approach. It may be a good idea to have bigger states. But regional parties based in linguistic states such as Akalidal in Punjab, DMK and AIDMK in Tamil Nadu, Asom Gana Parishad (AGP) etc are guided by regional considerations ignoring national interests.

The lack of homogeniety in the Indian population causes division between different sections of the people based on religion, region, language, caste and race. This has led to the use of political parties with agendas catering to one or a mix of these groups.

Member 1 If you had three apples and four oranges in one hand and four apples and three oranges in the other hand, what would you have?

Rashmi Very large hands.

Member 2 He ordered a cup of coffee for the candidate. Coffee arrived; kept before the candidate, then he asked what is before you?

Rashmi Instantly replied 'Tea'.

NOTE *Answer is correct because the question was "What is before you (U-alphabet), reply was "TEA" (T-alphabet Alphabet "T" was before Alphabet "U"*

Member 3 Miss Rashmi you hail from Kerala. Do you remember the tag line adopted by tourism department of Kerala for tourism promotion?

Rashmi Yes Sir, the tagline 'Kerala God's Own Country' was adopted by tourism department.

Member 4 Kerala is a famous tourist destination for domestic as well as international tourists. What is the reason for it?

Rashmi Sir, Kerala is an established destination for both domestic as well as foreign tourists. It is a state situated on the tropical Malabar coast of South Western India. It is also famous for its eco-tourism initiatives and beautiful backwaters. Kerala is unique in culture and traditions.

Chairman What is eco-tourism, Miss Rashmi? Why there is a need to take eco-tourism initiatives?

Rashmi Sir, the international eco-tourism society defines eco-tourism as "responsible travel that conserves the environment and improves the well-being of local people". Eco-tourism aims at preserving and sustaining the diversity of world's natural and cultural environments.

Member 3 Miss Rashmi, is clean energy related to eco-tourism?

Rashmi Not at all Sir, term clean energy is not related to eco-tourism. 'Clean energy' term is used in the context of production of electricity from sun, wind, waves and water by producing only a small amount of greenhouse gas in contrast to burning of fossil fuels like coal or oil to produce electricity which results in emission of greenhouse gases including CO_2 and methane.

Member 3 What is the future of solar energy in India? What is the function of the Centre for Solar Energy (CSE)?

Rashmi India is a country with huge solar energy potential due to its convenient location near the equator. India can generate over 1900 billion units of solar power annually which is enough to fulfil the entire annual power demand even in 2030.

Considering India's solar potential the government has rolled out various projects headed by the Centre for Solar Energy (CSE). The centre is involved in myriad functions such as techno economic and resource assessment, preparation of solar roadmaps, incentive structures etc.

The centre is actively engaged in guiding both the corporate and government sectors through various stages of project development for different solar technologies.

Member 2 Rashmi, some have criticised that the larger states are administratively unviable. The backwardness of UP, MP and Bihar is attributed to the enormous size of these states. Some have even suggested that the states should be abolished and we must have only districts. Don't you think your recommendation to have larger states runs counter to these views?

Rashmi You are quite right, Sir. However, I would like to submit that the suggestion to have districts and abolish the states has been made mainly to counter the linguistic phobia and sons-of-soil attitude. I am afraid the substitution of the present linguistic states by districts will not solve our problem. On the other hand, it will only create more problems. That is why I suggested that we should go back to large multi-lingual states.

Secondly, I also clarified that the states should be self-sufficient in natural resources and conform, if possible, to historical and natural boundaries. Lastly, the backwardness of UP, Bihar and MP is not because of their size. They were either zamindari system or princely states before the English annexed them. During British days, they had no industrial and commercial development on par with Bengal, Bombay and Madras Presidencies. With modern communication facilities and technological inputs they could be rapidly developed if only the political parties and vested interests would permit it.

The carving out of Uttarakhand from Uttar Pradesh, Jharkhand from Bihar and Chhattisgarh from Madhya Pradesh has hardly led to any material advancement of mother states. They still remain BIMARU states. Nor have the newly-created states benefited significantly except meeting the never-ending aspirations of politicians to enjoy political power at the cost of the nation. Crores of rupees have been spent in providing accommodation for Governors, Chief Minister, Ministers, bureaucrats and secretariat building, etc. Now there is a demand for further bifurcation of Uttar Pradesh between Western and Eastern Uttar Pradesh. The demands are endless.

Member 1 What steps did the Government of India take before demonetisation to lessen the hardship faced by the common man, small farmer etc pior to this bold step to curb black money?

Rashmi The first step was taken more than two years ago by starting the PMJDY (Jan Dhan Yojana) with zero balance bank accounts for the common man, small farmers, weaker sections etc. This scheme was started on 28th August, 2014 for financial inclusion of these sections of people. It enabled opening of more than 22 crores bank accounts during the last two years. After demonetisation, these people can deposit their old demonetised currency notes in their own bank accounts (up to a certain limit) without any penalty or income tax. Thus, the hardship due to demonetisation has been lessened for this section of Indian society.

Further, the small farmers have been benefited by issuing them Soil Health Cards, starting of the PM Krishi Sinchai Yojana to improve irrigation and the PM Fasal Beema Yojana for crop insurance. All these will benefit small farmers.

Member 2 Will demonetisation reduce corruption significantly?

Rashmi Demonetisation will not reduce corruption significantly because, at present, very few people hoard wealth in gunny bags full of bank notes. In today's world, there are refined ways of laundering money or stashing it away in *benami* properties, offshore bank accounts and foreign currency. Only the small fish keep their ill-gotten wealth in currency and the impact on black money will thus be very limited in the exercise. People indulging in large-scale corruption will not accept Indian currency as a bribe but take it in other forms.

Member 3 Will property prices come down due to demonetisation?

Rashmi Property prices went down in the past as the availability of the flats and houses increased and making transactions became difficult without PAN number. Also, as the PM announced, earlier the builders/sellers always asked part of the property price to be paid in cash (meaning that it will become black money). With demonetisation, the black money is out from the system at present. This has brought the property market almost to a standstill.

There will only be genuine buyers (with 100% white money) in the market for sometime to come. The government has put the nail in the coffin by starting investigations into *benami* properties. Thus, property prices will come down temporarily. But whether they will remain down is difficult to answer, as builders will work out methods to circumvent the rules sooner or later.

Member 4 Miss Rashmi on a serious note can you mention some of the major problems facing our country at this point of time?

Rashmi We have many problems facing us. The major ones are maintenance of the unity and integrity of the country, preservation of law and order, eradication of poverty, containing population explosion, removal of illiteracy, ensuring social justice, providing better deal for women and children and so on.

Member 5 What has been done so far for the safety and betterment of women in our country?

Rashmi Sir there have been no dearth of social, economic, political, legal and constitutional efforts made for empowerment of women by various governments. However, women in India continue to face atrocities such as rape, dowery killings, human trafficking, etc. Still much is needed to be done for women empowerment.

Chairman Do you feel that a short spell of military rule may help to resolve most of our problems faced by our country?

Rashmi Sir, I would like to submit by reservations on this point. Military rule elsewhere, like in Bangladesh, Pakistan, Afghanistan, Myanmar etc has not solved the problem. There is also possibility that once, military rule is allowed, it may continue for a long time and stop looking at people's interests. Our country is a democracy and this is the best political instrument for the development of our country. Only our politicians should not be self-centered.

Chairman Miss Rashmi, there are many neighbouring countries whose borders are shared by India. Comment upon the formation of SAARC.

Rashmi SAARC constitutes of Afghanistan, Bangladesh, Bhutan, Nepal, Maldives, Pakistan and Sri Lanka and the term refers to South Asian Association for Regional Cooperation (SAARC). These countries have similar cultures, social habits and economic problems. But all these countries face problems arising out of overpopulation, poverty, malnutrition, illiteracy, etc. It is believed that these countries of South Asia could progress fast only through cooperation with each other and by devising common plans for development. This concept led to the formation of the SAARC with the objective of mutual economic and social development.

Member 2 Who wrote a famous novel 'Train to Pakistan' on which a film was made later on?

Rashmi Sir eminent writer late Mr. Khushwant Singh wrote this novel.

Member 3 Have you read this novel?

Rashmi No Sir, I just saw the film 'Train to Pakistan' which was screened on TV also.

Member 4 Are you fond of watching Hindi movies?

Rashmi Not exactly Sir, I like to watch only some selected Hindi movies like 'Lagaan' or Chak de- India' or humourous one like 'Piku'.

Chairman Thank you very much Miss Rashmi. Now, we conclude this interesting and informative discussion. Do you want to ask any question for some sort of information from us?

Rashmi No Sir, I have no question. Thank you Sir.

Chairman You may leave now.

Rashmi Good day to all of you Sirs (She walks out smartly but without making any noise).

3. SAMPLE INTERVIEW FOR CIVIL SERVICES EXAMINATION (IPS)

Miss Arti Saxena is a postgraduate in Political Science from Delhi University. She is endowed with intellectual ability of a very high order. She is dressed in light almond coloured saree.

She is completely relaxed and entirely at ease in the company of the other candidates in the waiting room of the UPSC. With her pleasant smile and friendly temperament, she easily succeeds in creating a very favourable impact on the other candidates. She possesses the ability to argue convincingly. When her turn for interview comes, she takes leave of them in a cordial manner. She enters the interview room in a graceful style with complete confidence.

Arti Good Morning to you all Sirs. (With a smile and cheerful and audible voice).

Chairman Good Morning Miss Arti. Please take your seat. (She sits down on the chair meant for the candidate).

Chairman Miss Arti I find you have done your schooling in Dehradun and college education from Delhi. Would that mean that you have been out of your home state which you have mentioned as Punjab?

Arti Sir, my father belongs to Firozpur in Punjab and we have some land and an ancestral house in village nearby that city. My grandparents were there and now my paternal uncle resides there with his family. I have been to Firozpur with my parents on short visits. My father, who was in the Army has just retired as Brigadier. My parents now stay in Delhi where they have acquired a DDA flat. I was actually born at Wellington, Nilgiris, when my father was doing a course in staff college there. To ensure that my education did not suffer, my parents decided to put me at the Doon Public School in Deharadun.

Member 1 You said your father was in the army. Why did you not opt to join the army?

Arti Initially my parents were in favour of a career for me in the army. I was particularly keen on joining the Air Force and become a fighter pilot. But due to some personal reasons, my father didn't want me to join armed forces.

Chairman Miss Arti, your father is a defence officer. Could you tell us the role of Army in the country at the time of peace?

Arti The Army's primary duty is not just to fight wars, but also act as a deterrant. No country will dream of attacking someone with a strong army. Moreover, the army has a perpetual presence at borders to stop militants and other anti-national elements from sneaking into the country. The Army is regularly deployed in one or the other relief work in times of disasters like floods, earthquakes, tsunamis or other calamities. This was seen in Uttarakhand Disaster 2013 where the army saved a large number of civilians and was instrumental in bringing the area to normalcy.

Chairman How do you account for the continuing hold of the dowry evil despite it being legally banned? What can you do to fight the dowry menace as an IAS officer?

Arti Dowry is a deep-rooted social evil. Social reforms and changes cannot be achieved by legislation alone. Education, enlightenment, personal example by prominent people and economic betterment are necessary to bring about social reforms. The need and importance of legislative measures should also be stressed. We must do our best to arouse social consciousness against it.

As an IAS officer, I shall arrange for rigorous prosecution of those who give or accept dowry. I shall enlist the cooperation and help of the social organisations and educational institutions in my district to launch a vigorous campaign against the dowry evil. We can have dramas, street plays and folklore to spread our message. Promotion of education itself, especially among women and girls will go a long way in eradicating the evil of dowry.

Member 1 Miss Arti why do we need a campaign such as 'Beti Bachao Beti Padhao' initiated by the present government?

Arti Sir it is a very sad fact that inspite of all the development and in roads made by Indians, our girl child or daughters of India have been the victim of Indian male dominated society's mindset. Ours is a patriarchal society and every family wants a male heir. This rotten mindset has given rise to falling male-female ratio in our society. Even the educated people succumb to this infatuation with the male child. The project launched by Prime Minister Modi known as 'Beti Bachao Beti Padhao' is solely focussed on empowering of girl child.

Chairman Miss Arti how study of Political Science is going to help you to solve problems related to administration? Should study of Political Science be not restricted to politicians?

Arti Sir, Political Science focuses on the theory and practice of government and politics at the local, state, national and international levels. Political Science is dedicated to developing of understanding of various institutions practices and relations that constitute public life and modes of inquiry that promote citizenship. Sir Political Science is one subject that should be studied by every citizen including politicians. For an administrator study of Political Science can be of immense help by his awareness about democracy, socialism or welfare state, Fundamental Rights etc which study of political science can provide.

Member 2 There are two Houses of Parliament-Lok Sabha and Rajya Sabha. What does Rajya Sabha do or what is its role in our governance?

Arti Rajya Sabha is also known as the 'Council of the States' and it has its own distinctive features. In a vast country with immense diversities, a single directly elected House was considered inadequate to meet the challenges. Hence, it was decided to have federal system. Rajya Sabha has been created with different composition than Lok Sabha and method of election for its members is also different.

Rajya Sabha has its own role in the smooth running of government. Rajya Sahha enjoys certain special powers under the Constitution. All the subjects are divided into three lists-Union List, State List, and Concurrent List. If Rajya Sabha passes a resolution by a majority of two-third of its member present and it says that the certain resolution is necessary in the national interest, Parliament becomes empowered to make a law on the subject specified in the resolution.

Many finance bills and matters related to the budget must be passed both in Rajya Sabha and Lok Sabha.

Member 3 Who is the head of the police force?

Arti The head of the police force in a state is the Inspector General of Police called IG.

Member 3 Then this should mean that every district in a state should have a Deputy Inspector General of Police reporting to the IG, is it correct?

Arti Not exactly, Sir. In fact, a number of districts constitute a 'range'. The state is divided into convenient territories or ranges and the DIG has administrative control of a range or division.

Member 1 Have you heard about the 'third degree method' used by the police? What is meant by that?

Arti Sir, it is used by the police while interrogating criminals in which terror and violence is used to get to the truth. Sir, no criminal readily accepts the crime he has committed unless he is terrorised or frightened to some extent by the police.

Member 2 What is your opinion about the legality of the third degree method, especially in a democratic country like ours?

Arti Sir, this method of interrogation is not permitted under the law. In an ideal and modern society this method is not popular because by using third degree, the police sometimes forces people to admit or confess to crimes which they might not have committed. In my opinion, everyone is equal in the eyes of the law and a person should be treated as innocent until his or her crime is proved and there is no doubt left about his or her involvement.

Member 3 Then why should the police use this method for interrogating criminals?

Arti The police generally terrorises criminals mercilessly. This sometimes helps bring to book the right culprits as well as terrorise others who have not committed any crime. While I fully support the use of this method for hardened criminals, I am against its indiscriminate use.

Member 1 Miss Arti is there any controversy in India regarding superiority of legislature or judiciary? What are your views?

Arti The Indian Constitution is clear that proceedings in Parliament are not subject to judicial scrutiny. But because Indian Constitution has adopted both parliamentary and federal features, the controversy sometimes arises. Parliamentary form of government hints at legislative supremacy. But the federal nature of the Constitution makes it imperative that the highest judiciary is able to exercise the power of judicial review.

Member 1 Miss Arti, it is said that Political Science and History are closely related to each other. Can you throw some light on this point?

Arti Sir, it is totally true that both Political Science and History are mutually complementary and contributory. History provides material for Political Science. Political Science is studied in connection with the type of governance, a ruler was following, his policies, economic reforms if any. All these types of materials provide facts and data for Political Science.

Member 2 Secularism is one of the salient features of our Constitution. Can you name at least 10 words which relate to political, philosophical or economical aspect of human activities and end with 'ism'?

Arti Sir, it can be imperialism, socialism, conservatism, communalism, fanaticism, capitalism, nationalism, syllogism, casteism, monotheism etc.

Member 4 Miss Arti, there have been various election reforms in India from time to time. How will you assess present electoral system of India?

Arti Over the years, the Election Commission (EC) has conducted a number of laudable electoral reforms to strengthen democracy and enhance the fairness of elections. These reforms are quite adequate and admirable. Undoubtedly, the election machinery, under the aegis of the EC, deserves credit for conducting elections in a free and fair manner. However, our system is still plagued by many vices. To win votes, political parties resort to foul methods and corrupt practices. Such maladies encourage the anti-social elements to enter the electoral fray. The problem is not lack of laws, but lack of their strict implementation.

In order to stamp out these unfair tendencies, there is a need to strengthen the hands of the EC and to give it more legal and institutional powers. The EC must be entrusted with powers to punish the errant politicians, who transgress and violate the electoral laws.

Chairman What are your views, Miss Arti on Model Code of Conduct as envisaged by Election Commission of India?

Arti In every election, the EC issues a Model Code of Conduct for political parties and candidate to conduct elections in a free and fair manner. Model Code of Conduct lays down guidelines as to how political parties and candidate should conduct themselves during election. But despite the acceptance of the Code of Conduct by political parties, cases of its violations have been on the rise.

Member 4 Miss Arti many political problems stem from diversity in languages, religions, communities, ethnic groups and so on. What do you propose to overcome these problems?

Arti Sir, in my view instead of having states based on languages or religion we should have administrative zones or divisions which should be multi-lingual, multi-racial and multi-religious which may not be easily exploited by the politicians.

Chairman With the collapse of communism in the former Russia, would you say communism would meet the same fate in China, North Korea and other parts of the world?

Arti Yes Sir, the collapse of communism in Russia will have its fall out and even China is under pressure to grant freedom of expression and dissent to its citizens.

Member 2 Do you mean that with the collapse of communism in Eastern Europe and Russia, only democracy will prevail and the days of dictatorship have ended?

Arti Sir, the issue of democracy *vs* dictatorship should be considered independent of communism. Communism does not necessarily give rise to dictatorship. Other factors also can contribute to the rise of dictatorship as in the case of Nazi Germany. All I can say in that democracy is becoming increasingly popular at this point of time. If democratic governments fail to deliver the goods, other forms of government may arise, as has happened in many countries.

Member 3 Where do you think the strength of a political party lies in a great leader or a strong ideology?

Arti Sir, in my opinion, both are equally important. A great leader may help a political party in capturing votes but in the long run, it would be its party's ideology that would matter. Every party and its leader should try to work for the betterment of its people.

Member 2 Who is the first Indian woman who won the medal in Olympics in Badminton?

Arti Sir, Saina Nehwal is the first Indian woman to won a Bronze Medal in Olympics. She achieved this feat on 4th August, 2012 at London Olympics.

Member 1 Miss Arti, in a country with 1 : 22 billion population, achievements in sports by Indians is almost negligible. Why?

Arti Sir, many factors are responsible for this. India does not have good sports infrastructure and the rampant corruption that affects sports administration does not nurture the talents in a systematic manner. Moreover, physical fitness is the last priority of the most of the Indians. It is only very recently that elite Indians have started jogging rather than slowly walking in the parks. Another reason is poverty and malnutrition of large population which curtails the proper body growth and physical size.

Member 2 Miss Arti, do you pursue any hobby?

Arti Sir I am fond of listening old Indian music. Sometimes I indulge in cooking also. But as most of the time is spent in reading and preparing for the exam, I am unable to pursue any hobby.

Member 2 OK Miss Arti, your interview is over. Do you have any question to ask?

Arti No Sir, I don't have any question.

Chairman You may leave, Miss Arti.

Arti Thank you Sirs (Get up from her seat and gracefully exits closing the door behind her).

4. SAMPLE INTERVIEW FOR CIVIL SERVICES EXAMINATION (IFS)

Mr. Mohit Aggarwal is a candidate for the Indian Foreign Service. He is a postgraduate in English Literature from Presidency College, Kolkata. He is smartly dressed in shirt and brown tie. He looks distinguished. Without being over-dressed or casual, he is comfortably and correctly dressed.

When he is called for the interview, he walks with confidence and enters the interview room gracefully. He greets the Chairman and members of the board. Mr. Mohit Aggarwal takes a seat when he is asked by the Chairman to do so. He thanks everyone present. (He sits down smartly and with minimum of movement and noise. He remains relaxed but attentive).

Chairman I find from the relevant paper that you had been a student of the Presidency College, Kolkata. Can you tell us why it is named as Presidency College?

Mohit The Presidency College was the first college started in Bengal in its capital city of Calcutta (now Kolkata) by the British who were then ruling this country. In those days, Bengal, Bombay (now Mumbai) and Madras (now Chennai) were the three major presidencies of the sprawling British Indian empire. The British, who wanted to give their type of education to the Indians, started Presidency Colleges in all the three of their major presidencies.

Chairman When was this college upgraded to a status of full university? Who was the person behind this act?

Mohit Sir in 2010, under West Bengal's Chief Minister, Buddhadeb Bhattacharya, who was a former student of the college, it was upgraded to the status of a full university by the Presidency University Act, 2010.

Member 1 Bengal was quite advanced in industrial development at one stage. But today, it is lagging behind a lot in this sphere. How do you explain this setback?

Mohit When the Left Front led by CPI (M) was voted to power in West Bengal, the industrialists felt that the State Government might go in for nationalisation and would display antagonism against private enterprise.

Initially, the CPI(M) government did display such forebodings. Next, the labour became more militant. Naturally, the industry felt that the government would support the labour at the cost of the industry. Thirdly, acute power shortage gripped West Bengal which still persists. Next, the Central Government went slow with its industrial investments in West Bengal. These are the major factors which have contributed to the setback of industrial growth in West Bengal.

Chairman As I can see from your bio-data that you have done your post-graduation in English Literature. Some political parties are against the use of English language in India as they want more importance to be given to the use of regional language in India. What are your views on this, Mr Mohit?

Mohit Sir, in today's global world, the importance of English is immense. As it is an international language it is the most widely used language all over the world. Our country, which has so much diversity of regional languages, it would be appropriate to use English as a link language within the country.

Not only it is essential for international communications, it is far more easily accepted as a common language by a majority of Indians. Regional languages may be used within the states but use of English as a common language can't be ignored as it is the most important means of national integration. Moreover, more and more students go in for higher professional studies abroad in medicine, information technology and engineering. They need to be proficient in the use of English language.

Chairman Now, let us come to literature part. Do you regard literature as a common link between the people of various countries?

Mohit Sir, I feel that literature is related to a particular culture and often becomes the mirror of that society. It cannot serve as a common link between different people of diversified cultures in different countries. Literature at best represent the social, political, cultural and historical growth of a particular society at large.

Chairman But what about Shakespeare's or other writer's work having an universal appeal?

Mohit Sir, perhaps you did not get my point. I am not in favour of any geographical division of literature as such. All literature is universal in the sense that human characters any where in the world have same emotions, instincts or feelings and can not be restricted to any particular culture or society. But we cannot link people of various cultures on the basis of literature. They must have some other grounds to be linked to each other.

Member 2 Why do you want to serve in the Indian Foreign Service (IFS)?

Mohit Sir, the IFS is a highly prestigious and challenging service if you compare it with IAS, IPS and Allied Services. I had thought of joining the IFS right from when I entered college and so took courses in Japanese and French while completing my graduation. This is mentioned in my résumé. I am confident I will serve the government better with my knowledge of these languages as well as of English.

Chairman Explain what you understand by the Policy of Non-Alignment?

Mohit The background of the NAM (Non-Aligned Movement) was the world situation after the end of World War II. The world was then divided into two power blocs, the USSR and its allies on the left and USA and its allies on the right.

As more countries gained independence from colonisation by European countries, they did not want to join either of the power blocs. As they wanted to remain independent of any of these blocs, they organised a conference which took place from 18th-24th April 1955, in Bandung, Indonesia. In all, 29 countries representing more than half the world's population sent delegates to this conference. This set the ball rolling for the founding of NAM in 1961 at the next conference in Belgrade, Yugoslavia.

This movement adopted the Panchsheel (five principled) doctrine based on the Buddhist principles of mutual recognition, non-interference, non-aggression, mutual respect and peaceful coexistence. India was one of the founding members of NAM. At present NAM has 125 nations as its members. However, its significance has been diminished with the collapse of the USSR in 1991.

Member 1 You said that India was a founding member of NAM. Is India still a member?

Mohit Yes, Sir. India is still a member. When NAM was founded, the newly independent countries needed to form a group to assist each other. Since then, the world situation has been totally transformed and economic ties are more important than political alliances. That is why India has joined other alliances like SAARC, BRICS, BIMSTEC, etc as these are more relevant to the current world situation.

Member 2 As you want to join the IFS, you must be aware of the United Nations Organisation (UNO) and its role in the world. When was this organisation founded?

Mohit Sir, the United Nations charter was drafted at a conference in San Francisco, USA during April–June 1945; this charter took effect on 24th October, 1945, and the UN began operation. It was founded as an inter-governmental organisation to promote international cooperation. It was a replacement for the League of Nations, a largely ineffective body. It was established after World War II in order to prevent another such mass conflict.

Chairman Concepts like the First World, Second World and Third World are prevalent in international relations. Briefly explain what you know about the First World.

Mohit Sir, the industrialised capitalist countries of Western Europe, North America, Japan, Australia and New Zealand comprise the First World. In common parlance, "First World" refers to the rich nations of the world. The concept of First World was born during the Cold War (1950s to 1991) and included countries that were generally aligned with the West and opposed to the USSR.

They also included all NATO member countries. After the collapse of the USSR in 1991, the First World countries now are those countries with little political risk and a well functioning democracy, rule of law, a capitalist economy, economic stability and high standard of living.

Various ways in which modern First World countries are often determined include GDP, GNP, literacy rate and the Human Development Index.

Member 3 What is the role of an ambassador of a country?

Mohit The basic role of ambassador is to represent the interests of his country to foreign governments.

Member 3 Some countries are represented in India by their Ambassadors and some by their High Commissioners. What is the difference between the two? Our present envoy to the UK is our Ambassador of High Commissioner?

Mohit Sir, in the Commonwealth of Nations (an organisation comprising Great Britain and its former colonies), a High Commissioner is the most senior diplomat (generally ranking as an ambassador) in charge of the diplomatic mission of one Commonwealth government to another.

Thus, instead of an Embassy, the diplomatic mission is generally called a High Commission. This designation is rooted in history, when the nations were colonies of the British. There is no difference in rank between an Ambassador and a High Commissioner, as each of them is the most senior diplomat in charge of the diplomatic mission of that country in the host country.

Member 4 Why was EU created? What are its main aims? How many members does it have?

Mohit Sir, in the aftermath of World War II Europe was plagued by poverty, unemployment and economic instability. Initially European countries were assisted by USA in reviving their economies. Later on many European countries joined as a club to work together and promote economic and social progress, help people earn enough money and get treated fairly. The European Union (EU) started with just six countries, also called its members. At present, there are 28 member countries. When Britain ultimately exits from EU, there will be 27 member countries left.

Chairman Mr. Mohit, what do you understand by ASEAN Summit? Name some of the member countries. What are its aims?

Mohit The ASEAN (Association of South East Asian Nations) is a political-economic conglomeration of 10 member countries from South East Asia. 32nd ASEAN Summit was held in

Philippines in April, 2018. Some of its member countries are Indonesia, Malaysia, Myanmar, Cambodia, Laos etc.

Its aims include accelerating economic growth, social progress and socio-cultural evolution among its members, protection of regional peace and stability. It provides opportunities for member countries to resolve differences in a peaceful manner.

Member 1 Who is now world's oldest monarch?

Mohit Britain's Queen Elizabeth II became the world's oldest monarch after the death of king Abdullah of Saudi Arabia.

Chairman Mr. Mohit, if you are not selected for IFS, will you opt for any other allied services offered to you.

Mohit Sir, I am confident that I will be selected for Indian Foreign Services. If not selected this year, I will try next time, but I am sure to get into it.

Member 1 Do you have any hobbies, Mr. Mohit?

Mohit Sir, I do not have any specific hobby. But whenever I get spare time, I like to travel and go on trekking.

Member 2 Oh that's great, you travel in India or to some foreign destinations.

Mohit Sir, India is full of beautiful destinations. There is so much to travel inside India. In my childhood, I had the good luck to see many foreign countries as my father was in India Foreign Services. Now, I want to see as many places in India as I can.

Chairman Well done Mohit! Your interview is over, would you like to ask any question?

Mohit Thank you sir, but I don't have any questions right now.

Member OK Mr. Mohit, you may leave now. You can go to the next room and write a brief resume of our conversation.

Mohit Thank you Sirs (He now gets up and leaves the room quietly).

5. SAMPLE INTERVIEW FOR CIVIL SERVICES EXAMINATION (IRS)

Indian Revenue System (IRS) is the largest group of a Central Service amongst the organised Civil Services in the Government of India.

There are two streams of recruitment to the Indian Revenue Service : Direct Recruits and Promoted Officers. Direct recruits are selected from the prestigious Civil Services Exam conducted by UPSC and based on preferences opted by them.

Arjun Deshpande belongs to Maharashtra and is B.Com from Mumbai University. His eyes reflect warmth, friendliness and understanding. He has dressed himself in steel-grey trousers, dark blue shirt and a matching tie. He mixed up freely with other candidates and looks confident. When he is called for the interview he gives a gentle tap on the door for formal permission to enter the room. When he is allowed to enter, he proceeds towards the board members.

Arjun Good Morning to you all, Sirs.

Chairman Good Morning, Mr. Arjun. Please take your seat.

Arjun Thank your Sir (He occupies the chair meant for the candidate).

Chairman I find from your bio-data that you studied at the Mumbai University. OK What is so special about your city, Mumbai?

Arjun Sir, it is the financial capital of India. Moreover, it is the biggest city where thousands of people related to Bollywood live and earn their living. Mumbai is also a centre for cotton textiles.

Member 1 OK Mr. Arjun who all are there in your family?

Arjun Sir, I have my parents and one elder brother who is a colonel in Indian Army. My father is a businessman and owns a cotton textile mill in Mumbai.

Chairman You could have joined your father's business. Why do you want a government job?

Arjun Sir, I wanted to do something different. My father is a busy man, he does not get much time for family. My brother gets posted at non-family station so he is rarely able to spend time with family.

I thought of applying for a government job which might provide an opportunity to be with family in normal circumstances.

Chairman Do you mean to say Mr. Arjun government jobs do not keep any one busy?

Arjun I never meant this way, Sir, but I think out of three choices; business, defence and civil services, I might get some time to relax with my family.

Member 1 OK you belong to Maharashtra. Can you tell us Mr. Deshpande which is state bird of Maharashtra state?

Arjun Sir, yellow footed green pigeon, is a state bird of our state.

Chairman Which is the extreme/southern district of Maharashtra?

Arjun Sir, Sindhudurg is the extreme Southern district of Maharashtra.

Member 2 Where is 'Uran Project' initiated in Maharashtra?

Arjun Uran is part of Navi Mumbai city on the Western coast of India. It lies in the Raigad district, East of Mumbai across the Dharamtar Creek. Uran is primarily a fishing and agriculture village which has developed into the Special Economic Zone (SEZ) of Uran.

Member 3 Have you heard of Bombay Presidency, Mr. Arjun?

Arjun Yes Sir, Bombay Presidency was a former province of British India which later included much of Western and Central India as well as parts of Pakistan and the Arabian Peninsula.

Chairman OK coming to your subject, can your explain Direct taxes and Indirect taxes?

Arjun Sir, Direct taxes are directly paid to the Government of India by the tax payers. Income tax, wealth tax and corporation tax are examples of direct taxes. Indirect taxes are applied on the manufacture or sale of goods and services.

Member 2 How can we differentiate between commerce, trade and business?

Arjun Sir, commerce is the activity of buying and selling of goods or services especially on a large scale or quantity. Trade means buying and selling. It is the exchange of goods and services among buyer and seller in which both the parties are benefitted.

Business refers to those economic activities which are connected with the production or purchase and sale of goods or supply of services with the main objective of earning profit.

Member 2 Can you mention some of the major problems being faced by our countrymen at this point of time?

Arjun Sir, according to me some major problems India facing at present is population growth, pollution, deteriorating infrastructure in business, education and healthcare; graft and corruption. Sir India's population is growing 20% per decade leading to problems which include food deficiency, sanitation and pollution. India uses coal for 80% of its power requirements and it has been slow to transition to cleaner energy sources. Indians involved in agriculture have the least access to basic education and healthcare necessities. Corruption is widespread and has rather become a way of life.

Member 1 Mr. Deshpande is there any difference in being an IAS officer and an IRS officer?

Arjun Sir, IRS officers are concerned with the compilation, administration and policy formation of direct and indirect taxes. Due to this, IRS officers are often called as Tax Administrators of India. An IAS officer is a top ranked official in the civil service of the executive division of the Government of India. In their daily affairs, IAS officers carry out administration and policy works at national level.

Member 1 Tell me what is a Service tax?

Arjun Sir, Service tax is an indirect tax imposed by the government on service providers on certain service transactions, but is actually paid by the customers. Services provided by air conditioned restaurants and short term accommodation provided by hotels, inns, etc are included in the taxable services.

Chairman Can you explain accrual system with an example?

Arjun Yes, Sir accrual accounting is a method that measures the performance and position of a company by recognising economic events regardless of when cash transaction occur. e.g. when a company sells a TV to a customer who uses a credit card, the revenue generated by the sale of TV by accrual method recognises the TV sale at the point at which the customer buys the TV. Even though cash isn't yet in the bank, the sale is booked to an account known in accounting language as 'accounts receivable' increasing the seller's revenue.

Chairman Arjun what do you understand by 'Assessment Year?'

Arjun Assessment Year is the period that starts from 1st April and ends on 31st March. It is the year immediately succeeding the financial year wherein the income of the previous financial year is assessed.

Member Under how many heads an individual's income is categorised?

Arjun There are five main heads under which an individual's income is categorised. They are salaries, income from house property, profits and gains of business or profession, capital gains and income from other sources.

Chairman Can you tell us something about the Taxation Principles?

Arjun Taxation Principles are the basic concepts by which a government is meant to be guided in designing and implementing an equitable taxation regime.

Member 1 What more has been called the 'Surgical Strike' within India to curb black money?

Arjun Indian Prime Minister Mr. Narendra Modi, in an address to nation announced that ₹ 500, ₹ 1000 notes will cease to be legal tender from midnight 8th November, 2016, demonetisation drive has been taken out to root out menace of black money, corruption and fake currency from country.

Chairman What is GST? How it is going to benefit the country?

Arjun Sir, GST is a consumption tax that is collected on sale of manufactured goods and services. Since it is a consumption tax, it is passed on until the last stage, where in the customer bears the tax, just like excise duty is imposed. GST is called the biggest tax reform as it simplifies tax structure, increases tax compliance, increases government revenue and will integrate states.

Member 1 Do you think that the government's policy of relaxing the controls on the private sector, has paid off?

Arjun Yes Sir, I definitely think so, the relaxation of controls has enabled the private sector to increase production and export substantially within a short period.

Member 2 Don't you think that this policy of relaxation of controls over the private sector goes against our socialistic concept?

Arjun Sir, I would disagree with you on the issue. Sir, in my opinion socialism means and implies the sharing of wealth and not sharing the poverty. The tight and unimaginative restrictions and controls on private sector result in industrial stagnation and we have inflation, unemployment and increasing poverty. The relaxation over the private sector will help in industrial growth.

Chairman Well, Mr. Arjun, what do you understand by the term 'globalisation?'

Arjun Sir, globalisation implies the opening of local and nationalistic perspectives to a broader outlook of an interconnected and independent world with free transfer of capital, goods and services across national frontiers.

Member 1 Mr. Arjun do you have any hobby? What do you do in your spare time?

Arjun Sir, I am fond of reading newspaper and magazines. Sometimes I indulge myself in cooking also.

Member 2 Cooking, isn't it strange hobby? What do you love to cook?

Arjun Sir cooking is not a strange hobby. All the good chefs in five star hotels must be passionate about cooking. Moreover, cooking relaxes my nerves and I feel very happy whenever my prepared dish turns out to be tasty and well-cooked. I love making soups and Chinese and Italian dishes.

Chairman Thank you very much Mr. Arjun. Now we conclude this very interesting and informative discussion. Do you want to ask any question for some sort of information from us?

Arjun No Sir, I have no question.

Chairman You may leave now.

Arjun Thanks to all of you Sirs (Gets up quietly and walks out of the room confidently).

6. SAMPLE INTERVIEW FOR SSB INTERVIEW (ARMY/NAVY/AIR FORCE)

SSB i.e. Service Selection Board is the personality and intelligence interview spread over 5 days. The test conducted by SSB aims at selecting individuals with OLQ (Officer like Qualities). During this process personal interview can be conducted any day either 2nd, 3rd or 4th day of the interview procedure.

Aakash Srivastava completed his graduation from Hindu College. He has been called for the interview just after the completion of the GTO task. Hence, he does not get the time to dress himself for the interview. When he is called for the interview he walks with firm steps and full confidence towards the interview room. He gets in after gently knocking at the door and waiting for a few seconds at the entrance. He comes to a halt when he comes near the chair meant for the candidate, springs to attention position and proceeds to greet the chairman and other members.

Aakash Good afternoon, Sirs.

Chairman Good afternoon Mr. Aakash. Please be seated and feel comfortable.

Aakash Thank you very much Sir (He occupies the chair meant for the candidate).

Chairman From your bio-data I could see that you have been born and brought up in Delhi. From where you did your schooling? What about your college?

Aakash Sir, I passed my 10th and 12th from DPS, RK Puram, New Delhi. I did my graduation (B.Sc) from Hindu College affiliated with Delhi University.

Member 1 Who was the founder of Hindu College? When was it founded. What is its importance in India's freedom struggle?

Aakash Sir, Hindu College was founded more than a century ago in 1899 by Late Shri Krishan Dassji Gurwale. In the back drop of the nationalist struggle against British rule, some prominent citizens including Sir Gurwaleji, decided to start a college that would while being non-elitist and non-sectarian, provide nationalist education to the youth. Hindu College became a centre for intellectual and political debate during India's freedom struggle, especially during the Quit India Movement.

Chairman From your bio-data I find that you are having a brilliant academic record. I think with this record you could have chosen any other career. Then why do you want to join Indian Army.

Aakash Sir, I feel in today's competitive environment it is very difficult to get a job of your choice. In these circumstances, the job which gives you maximum satisfaction is the best job for you. Service in Army has been my passion since my childhood. I am inclined towards this career because it is among the few profession in which, direct service to humanity is called for. This profession will bring out the best in me.

Chairman What are your hobbies?

Aakash Sir, I am fond of collecting stamps. In outdoor activities I used to play cricket with my friends. I am also interested in reading novels.

Chairman Who is your favourite author?

Aakash Sir, I like the fictions of Sidney Sheldon.

Chairman What is the constitution of the Armed Forces of India?

Aakash The supreme command of the Armed Forces is vested in the President of India. The responsibility for national defence, however, rests with the Cabinet. All important questions having a bearing on defence are decided by the Cabinet Committee on political affairs, which is presided over by the Prime Minister. The Defence Minister is responsible to Parliament for all matters concerning the Defence services. The Ministry of Defence comprises of three departments (i) Department of Defence, (ii) Department of Defence Production and Supplies and (iii) Department of Defence Research and Development. The administrative and operational control of the Armed Forces is exercised by the Department of Defence and the three service headquarters of the Army, Navy and Air Force. India has the second largest Army, the fourth largest Air Force and the sixth largest Navy in the world.

Chairman What qualities should a defence officer have?

Aakash Sir, I feel besides being a good leader, defence officer should have good communication skills, resourcefulness, initiative, cooperative attitude, emotional stability and intelligence in a proper proportion.

Chairman Can you name the Gallantry Awards instituted by the Government of India?

Aakash Sir, the Government of India has instituted four Gallantry Awards. The highest award is the Param Vir Chakra, then the Maha Vir Chakra and the Vir Chakra. The fourth, the Ashoka Chakra, was instituted for the non-combatants.

Chairman Who makes the recommendations for the Gallantry Awards?

Aakash These are made by Central Honours and Awards Committee.

Chairman Who are its member?

Aakash It comprises the Defence Minister who is its Chairman, the Defence Secretary and the three service chiefs. The Prime Minister or the President gives the final approval for the award.

Chairman Can you name some branches of the Indian Army?

Aakash Some of the important branches of the Indian Army include the Infantry, the Army Ordinance Corps, the Signal Corps, the Tank Corps and the Army Medical Corps.

Member 1 Mr. Aakash, what is India's defence policy?

Aakash Sir our Armed Forces are there to defend the country from any foreign invasion, but India has no desire to capture the territory of any other country. Our country is peace-loving and believes in peaceful co-existence. But after facing many aggression, India wants to be self-sufficient in defence material production so that our dependance on other countries for defence equipment and materials remains at the minimum. The launch of Defence Procurement Policy is aimed at boosting India's target of 'Make in India' policy besides creation of major domestic defence industry to cater to its own needs as well as exports.

Member 1 What are the functions of civil defence?

Aakash Civil defence measures are designed to deal with immediate emergency conditions, protect the public and restore vital services and facilities that have been destroyed or damaged by disaster. Some support emergency services rendered by Civil Defence are rescue operations, fire fighting, law enforcement, medical care, public work's repair and provision of voluntary food, shelter and clothing.

Member 1 Do you think, Mr. Aakash that introduction of National Service Scheme's (NSS) in educational institutions arouses patriotism in today's youths?

Aakash I don't think so, as patriotism is something inherent in a person. But introduction of NSS in educational institution was because Gandhiji wanted the students to understand their social responsibility and always give priority to this. The Education Commission headed by Dr. DS Kothari (1964-66) recommended that students at all stages of education should be associated with some form of social service. After the launch of the NSS programme in various universities and + 2 level school, a general awareness has grown in students towards the realities of life and appreciation of the problems of the people.

Member 2 What is the Right to Freedom of speech provided in our Indian Constitution?

Aakash Sir, Freedom of Speech is one part of the Fundamental Rights of a citizen under the head 'Right to Freedom'. Article 19 of the Constitution guarantees freedom under this right. The freedom is subject to reasonable restrictions that may be imposed by the state in the national interest.

Member 2 Army has its role not only during war but during peace time also. Can you throw light on this statement?

Aakash Yes Sir, there are a lot of work which Army keeps doing during peace time. Its training schedules continue during peace time as it is said that 'the more you sweat in peace, the less you bleed in battle'. Army units keep undergoing exercises in desert areas, mountain warfare, etc. Moreover the indestructible presence of army on the border ensures complete safety of the country by safeguarding our borders. Whenever the country faces any disaster, it is the army which comes to the rescue of people, be it landslide, earthquake, floods or Tsunamis. National Security Guard (NSG) is the force from Indian Armed forces that take care of security issues and save public from any internal threats like riots, terrorist attack, etc.

Member 2 Is India self-sufficient in producing defence equipment at present?

Aakash Sir, at present we are not 100% self-sufficient in producing defence equipment. But Defence Research and Development Organisation (DRDO) is committed to make India self-sufficient in producing defence equipment ranging from missiles, manned and unmanned aircrafts to sensors among others. It is depending on the indigenisation of the weapon system. Five missions have been planned to make sure that India has cutting edge capabilities in defence production.

Member 2 Mr. Aakash, can you give examples of stored energy? Will you include nuclear energy in this category?

Aakash Sir potential energy, electrical energy, chemical energy all are examples of stored energy, but nuclear energy cannot be called stored energy as it is obtained by breaking a heavy nucleus into light nucleus of comparable masses. It can also be obtained by the formation of a heavy nucleus due to fusion of two light nuclei.

Chairman Which is the indigenously built stealth fighter, being inducted in Indian Air Force?

Aakash 'Tejas' is the single engine supersonic delta wing aircraft, which is inducted by IAF. The aircraft is developed by Hindustan Aeronautics Limited (HAL) and Aeronautical Development Agency (ADA). The aircraft is capable of four tonnes of weapons and firing air-to-air missiles and laser guided bombs to attack enemy fighters and his ground targets at a speed of more than 1300 kms per hour. The induction of the fighter will give a major boost to IAF's fighting.

Member 1 Will you come back again, Mr. Aakash for SSB interview if you fail this time?

Aakash Sir, I think I will be able to make it this time only. If by chance, I am not selected, I will definitely try it again and again, till I am selected.

Chairman Good confidence, Mr. Aakash, we wish you the very best.

Aakash Thank you Sir.

Chairman Well Mr. Aakash, it was really nice talking to you on a variety of issues. Should we call it a day?

Aakash Thank you very much Sirs, (He wishes the President and the members and leaves the room).

7. SAMPLE INTERVIEW FOR SSB INTERVIEW (ARMY/NAVY/AIR FORCE)

Shashank Chaudhary is a science graduate and belongs to Faridabad, a city in Haryana. This is his first attempt in SSB. He has performed well in psychological tests in GTO tests and satisfied with his performance. Since he was told to appear for the interview in the evening, he has dressed himself in white shirt and grey trousers. A navy blue tie makes his formal dress more appealing. His eyes reflect his keenness, confidence and determination. He appears relaxed and at ease while waiting outside the interview room. When his name is called for the interview, he walks towards the interview room with confidence takes a formal permission before entering the room. After the permission is granted, he walks towards the chair meant for the interviewee.

Shashank Good evening, Sirs.

Chairman Good evening Shashank, please take your seat.

Shashank Thank you very much, Sir (He follows the instruction and takes his seat).

Chairman Mr. Shashank, from your bio-data, I can see, you were educated in many institutions of UP. Don't you find that UP is a comparatively backward state?

Shashank Yes Sir, it is comparatively backward due to its large population and its size.

Chairman What about the standard of education in UP?

Shashank Sir there are several famous universities and affiliated colleges in UP. It can boast of two IIT's at Kanpur and Varanasi, IIM in Lucknow which provide quality education. Even the standard of education in government run schools is pretty good.

Chairman Mr. Shashank why do you want to join Armed Forces? You have given choice for Air Force? Can you state the reason?

Shashank Sir, my grandfather and father all are in Armed Forces. I have been born and brought up in an atmosphere of discipline and patriotism. Moreover I have been infatuated by the personality and status of defence officers. My choice of Indian Air Force is mainly because I wanted to experience a different field, other than Army and still be called a man in uniform. I also think that as a defence officer he/she is in a better and stronger position to serve your motherland.

Member 1 Mr. Shashank, you appear to be quite fresh even after 3 days of continuous and gruelling testing?

Shashank Sir, that's the true test of an officer in the making continuous and gruelling testing should not tire a defence officer as during the war or in peaceful operations he may have to strain himself for days together without getting proper rest or food.

Member How do you like this city of Mysuru?

Shashank Sir, I am visiting this garden city of India for the first time. I find it one of the most beautiful cities alongwith its rich cultural heritage.

Member 1 Can you tell us the historical significance of the State of Karnataka?

Shashank Sir, Karnataka has a glorious heritage of over two thousand years. The great Vijayanagara Empire and the Bahmani Kingdoms flourished here in medieval age. In the modern history, the great Tipu Sultan of Mysore evokes feelings of patriotism in every human soul. The State of Karnataka, constituted as Mysore under the States Reorganisation Act, 1956, bought together the Kannada speaking people distributed in five states and consisted of the territories of the old states of Mysore and Coorg, the Bijapur, Kanara and Dharwar districts and the Belgaum district. Earlier known as Mysore, the state was renamed Karnataka in 1973.

Member 2 You have mentioned in your bio-data that you have represented your college team as a captain in inter-university level. Do you agree that the performance of a captain as a batsman and a bowler suffer under the pressure of captaincy?

Shashank Sir, I agree that the captain has to carry an extra-psychological pressure which basically relates to the outcome of the game and the pressure becomes more intense when any team passes through a lean patch. But to allow this pressure to affect your performance in the game is something that differs from individual to individual. The main task of the captain is to lead the whole team as a cohesive unit and to motivate each member by encouraging his performance. Moreover, it is the strong mindset of a captain which is his biggest asset.

Member 2 What will be the future of the five days Test match in view of the increasing popularity of the One-day Cricket and T20 matches?

Shashank The Test matches have their own charm and there are many cricket lovers who are enthusiastic supporters of these Test matches. I therefore, feel that the Test matches will continue to survive. As regards the players themselves, they gain valuable experience, patience and training in the various departments of the game when they play the Test lasting for five days.

Member 1 Who is the Supreme Commander of the defence forces? Who is responsible for defending the nation?

Shashank Sir, the Supreme Commander of the defence forces is vested in the President of India. However, the responsibility for national defence rests with the cabinet and the government.

Member 1 Mr Shashank tell us how many commands are there in the Indian Army and which are those?

Shashank Sir, the Indian Army now has six commands. Earlier there were only five commands i.e. the Western command, Eastern command, Northern command, Southern command and the Central command. Now, a sixth command has been added which is called the Training command.

Chairman What are the ranks of the people who are head of each command?

Shashank Sir each command is under the control of a General Officer Commanding in Chief of the rank of Lt General.

Member 2 How many commands are there in Indian Air Force? Who heads each of the commands?

Shashank Sir the Indian Air Force has five operational commands each of which is headed by an AOC-in-C (Air Officer Commander-in-Chief) with the rank of Air Marshal.

Chairman Where is Indian Air force headquarters located?

Shashank Indian Air force headquarters is located in New Delhi which is commanded by the Chief of Air Staff.

Member 1 Lowest commissioned rank in army is second Lieutenant. What are its equivalent rank in Indian Navy and Indian Air Force?

Shashank Sir, the lowest commissioned rank in the Navy is Acting Sub-Lieutenant and in the Air Force it is Pilot-Officer.

Chairman India has achieved a self-reliance in producing missiles. Can you tell us the name of Indian missiles and their properties?

Shashank Sir, the Defence Research and Development Department in the Ministry of Defence looks after the development and research programmes and requirements of the armed forces. It has under it Defence Research and Development Organisation and 50 laboratories. The Defence Research and Development Laboratory (DRDL) has developed and successfully test-fired five missiles. These are

- **Prithvi** It is the India's first indigenously built missile. It is tactical surface-to-surface missile. It has a range capability of 250 km with different types of warheads facilities. It was first test-fired on 25th February, 1988 from Sriharikota. Prithvi was inducted into the Indian Army in 1993.
- **Trishul** It is a short-range two level quick reaction surface to air missile. When fully developed, it will be used by all the three forces-Army, Air Force and Navy against low flying objects. It has a range of 5 metres to 9 km. It was first tested in 1988.
- **Agni** It is an international range ballistic surface-to- surface missile with range capability upto 2500 km. It was tested for the first time in 1989.
- **Akash** It is the most modern multitarget surface to air missile designed to defend large installations like oil fields against enemy air attacks. It has a range capacity of 25 km. It was successfully test launched in 1990.
- **Nag** It is an anti-tank guided missile of the 'fire and forget' type having a range capability of 4 km.

It has been developed to counter contemporary advances in tank armour. It is the most advanced missile of its kind in the world. First test flight was made in 1988.

Chairman How does Indian Air Force help during national disasters?

Shashank The Indian Air Force along with the other branches of Indian Armed Forces provide assistance in disaster relief such as during natural calamities by undertaking evacuation or search and rescue operations and air dropping relief supplies in affected areas. The IAF provided extensive assistance to relief operations during Gujarat cyclone in 1998, the tsunami in 2004 and floods in North India in 2013.

Member 1 What was the name of the operation carried on by Indian Air Force to provide relief to flood affected people in Uttarakhand and Himachal Pradesh in 2013?

Shashank Sir, it was called 'Operation Rahat'. In a bid to evacuate people and rescue operation in the badly affected area of Uttarakhand and Himachal Pradesh, by heavy rains, the Indian Air Force launched this operation.

Chairman Mr. Shashank are you interested in any sports? What games do you play?

Shashank Sir, I play squash, tennis and badminton. As regards other sports, I have taken part in atheletics. I have participated in long distance race and swimming. I am also interested in watching tennis matches on TV specially the international ones.

Member 2 Do you pursue any hobby?

Shashank Sir, I am fond of growing vegetables in my kitchen garden. This hobby I developed only after completing my school education, when I started living with my parents at Faridabad where we have got a cottage and a huge kitchengarden.

Member 2 Do you cook also?

Shashank Sir, not much, but my mother has taught me some basic cooking like making dal and rice or pulao so that in emergency, I may not remain hungry.

Chairman Good, Mr. Shashank, your interview is over. You may leave now. (He offers Shashank for the handshake).

Shashank Thank you very much Sirs (He responds with a warm hand shake with the firm grip and says goodbye).

8. SAMPLE INTERVIEW FOR BANK PO

S Sukumar has graduated in Electronic Communication (B. Tech). He was called in for an interview for PO from SBI Bank. He is wating for the call for interview in waiting hall with relaxed posture. When his name is called for interview, he walks with confidence towards the interview room and seeks permission to enter.

Sukumar Good morning Sirs.

Chairman Good morning Mr. Sukumar, please take your seat.

Sukumar Thank you Sir (Takes his seat and sits confidently).

Chairman Mr. Sukumar, you are an Engineer. Before we proceed further, please introduce yourself.

Sukumar Sir, I am Siddharth and resident of Delhi. After doing 10+2, I got admitted in Electronic Communication course. After graduation, I joined Infosys in 2011.

Chairman Your marks in 10+2 and Engineering suggest that you have been a sincere student. You got a technical degree and a good placement in a reputed IT company. However, you did not opt for continuing the IT job.

Sukumar No doubt, Infosys is a reputed IT company, but I always aspired to shape my career in banking service.

Member 1 What is handshaking?

Sukumar Sir, in information technology, telecommunications and related fields, handshaking is an automated process of negotiation, that dynamically sets parameters of a communications channel established between two entities before normal communication over the channel begins. It follows the physical establishment of the channel and precedes normal information transfer.

Member 1 OK Mr Sukumar. Now, tell me about RBI's objective in setting up 'payment banks'.

Sukumar The objective behind creating payment banks is to bring about financial inclusion, by making it easier for anyone to get a bank-account. The aim is to provide bank accounts to people in the villages, to bring them into digital economy, to send money, buy goods and services through the digital economy. The new payment banks will also make people less dependent on cash.

Member 1 What is a current account in a bank? Are there any specific conditions to open a current account?

Sukumar Sir, it is a type of bank account on which a customer may draw cheques up to the amounts of the credit balance in the account, or beyond it to an agreed overdraft limit. Sir, there are no specific conditions to open a current account. These are basically meant for businessmen and are never used for the purpose of investment or savings.

Member 2 What is NABARD? Why it was set up?

Sukumar Sir, NABARD is the National Bank for Agriculture and Rural Development. It was set up in July, 1982. NABARD was set up to act as refinancing institution for agriculture and rural production units. Its purpose is to expand and strengthen the structure of rural credit including the finance to cottage and small scale units.

Member 2 Have you heard of Kisan Credit Card Scheme? What exactly this facility is?

Sukumar Sir, with a view to make credit easily available to farmers, the government introduced Kisan Credit Card Scheme in 1998-99 to facilitate access to credit from Commercial Banks and Regional Rural Banks. The scheme has been taken up by 27 Commercial Banks, 183 Central Cooperative Banks and 144 Regional Rural Banks for implementation.

Member 2 What is the purpose behind setting up regional rural banks?

Sukumar Sir Regional Rural Banks (RRB) were established under the provisions of an ordinance promulgated on 26th September, 1975 with an objective to ensure sufficient institutional credit for agriculture and other rural sectors. These banks mobilise financial resources from rural and semi-urban areas and grant loans and advances mostly to small and marginal farmers, agricultural labourers and rural artisans.

Chairman What do you understand by private banking?

Sukumar Banking services offered to high net worth individuals is called private banking. Financial institutions offering private banking earn commission by providing quality assistance to their high net worth customers in investing their money. By private, we mean that the services are provided and tailored on a more personal basis.

Chairman What is PIN or Personal Identification Number?

Sukumar PIN is the numeric password which is separately mailed or handed over to the customers by the bank while issuing a debit or credit card. Most banks require the customers to change the PIN on the first use for security reasons. Without PIN one cannot do any financial transactions.

Member 2 Have you heard of RTGS system, Mr Sukumar? Is there any minimum/maximum amount stipulated for RTGS transactions?

Sukumar RTGS stands for Real Time Gross Settlement, which can be defined as the continuous real-time settlement of funds transfers individually on an order by order basis (without netting). 'Real Time' means the processing of instructions at the time they are received rather than at some later time. 'Gross Settlement' means the settlement of funds transfer instructions occurs individually. Considering that the funds settlement takes place in the books of the Reserve Bank of India, the payments are final and irrevocable.

The RTGS system is primarily meant for large value transactions. The minimum amount to be remitted through RTGS is ₹ 2 lakh. There is no upper ceiling for RTGS transactions.

Member 1 Who is Banking Ombudsman? Does he really help the customers?

Sukumar The Banking Ombudsman is a senior official appointed by Reserve Bank of India to redress customer complaints against deficiency in certain banking services. Yes, if the customer's complaint is genuine and fulfills all the conditions for making a complaint, the banking Ombudsman will resolve the issue.

Member 2 What is Forex market?

Sukumar Sir, the Forex or Foreign Exchange market is the 'place' where currencies are traded. Currency exchange is a must to conduct foreign trade and business.

Member 2 How does 'Forex' market differ from other markets?

Sukumar Sir, unlike stocks, futures or options, currency trading does not take place on a regulated exchange. It is not controlled by any central governing body. There are no clear houses to guarantee the trades. Participants in this market compete and cooperate with each other.

Member 1 What are open market operations?

Sukumar Sir, buying and selling of government securities and bonds in open market by government are called open market operations. Its purpose is to maintain desired liquidity levels.

Member 2 Mr Kumar, have you heard of 'World Bank'? How does it help developing countries?

Sukumar Sir, the World Bank is an international financial institution. It comprises two institutions the International Bank for Reconstruction and Development (IBRD) and International Development Association (IDA).

The World Bank is a vital source of financial and technical assistance to developing countries around the world. It offers support to developing countries through policy advice, research and analysis and technical assistance.

Chairman What are NPA or Non-Performing Assets?

Sukumar The assets of a bank which do not perform or do not bring any return are called Non-Performing Assets. NPA is a credit facility in respect of which the interest or principle payment has not been paid for more than 90 days. NPA results from bad loans or defaults.

Member What are the problems that are caused by NPAs?

Sukumar If NPAs reflect badly in a bank's account books and adversely impact the national economy. Some other problem caused by NPAs can be that the depositors do not get rightful returns, bank shareholders are adversely affected and liquidity problems are faced by the banks.

Chairman Do you play any sports, Mr Sukumar?

Sukumar Yes Sir, I play football at least on weekends. I am also fond of watching football games at TV.

Chairman Mr Sukumar, your interview is over. Would you like to ask any question?

Sukumar No Sir, Thank you very much Sir.

Member You may leave now.

Sukumar Thank you Sir, (Gets up and leaves the room quietly).

9. SAMPLE INTERVIEW FOR BANK PO

Sneha Rastogi belongs to Meerut, a town in UP. She has completed B.Com from Meerut University. She is endowed with intellectual ability of a very high order, robust common sense and sharp features. She is dressed in white suit with violet embroidery. She is completely relaxed and entirely at ease in the company of the other candidates in the waiting room. She has a good command on English language. When her name is called for interview, she leaves her fellow candidates and walks confidently towards interview room. She enters the room after formal knocking at the door with confidence.

Chairman Yes, please come in Miss Sneha.

Sneha Thank you Sir and good morning to all of you, Sirs.

NOTE *If the panel also comprises of a lady interviewer, after wishing above, you can wish her by saying "Good Morning ma'am".*

Chairman Good Morning Sneha; please be seated.

Sneha Thank you Sir. (She occupies the chair nicely, without pulling or dragging it).

Chairman Sneha in which subject you have completed your graduation.

Sneha Sir, I did B.Com and Mathematics, Accountancy and English were my subjects.

Chairman Your father is a lecturer in English. Why didn't you think of a similar career for yourself?

Sneha I have a liking for Maths and Accounts since Matriculation. I got my maximum marks in Maths in the Board Examinations in 10th and 12th classes. My parental uncle who is a Chief Manager in the State Bank of India advised me to go for B.Com seeing my liking for the pertinent subjects. So here I am, Sir.

Chairman OK. Miss Sneha, can you define the term Double Entry System in accounts?

Sneha It is a system of recording a debit and a credit for an entry. It follows that for every debit there is a credit and a credit for every debit.

Chairman What is a Balance Sheet?

Sneha It is the statement of the balances of all the accounts of a firm or a company as on a particular date depicting its financial position as on that date.

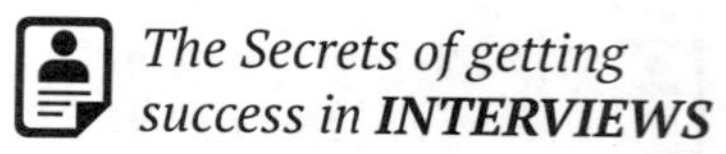

Chairman Should the Profit and Loss Account of that company can be of the same date?

Sneha No Sir, the Profit and Loss Account is not for a particular date. It is a particular period, say a half year or a year.

Chairman OK, but why is it so?

Sneha Sir, the Profit and Loss Account is for a period, say a financial year, to show what the business has done during that period; whether it has earned a profit, and if so, how much, or whether it has suffered a loss, and if so, how much. The Balance Sheet is as on a particular date; say 31st March of the year, to show the detail of the assets and liabilities of a company, i.e. its financial position as on that date.

(The Chairman is done with his questions and the interview passes on to the 1st Member)

Comments The candidate has made a good initial impression on the Board. She has not only shown good manners but also self-confidence. She seems to have chosen the profession on the basis of her interest and aptitude; not mere desire. She is able to answer the questions correctly which shows that he has prepared well.

Member 1 What do you understand by LIBOR and SIBOR?

Sneha Sir, LIBOR is London Inter Bank Offered Rate while SIBOR is Singapore Inter Bank Offered Rate.

Member 1 Which is the largest bank in India?

Sneha It is the State Bank of India, Sir both in terms of number of branches and the amount of deposits and also among public sector banks and private sector banks.

Member 1 Can you tell me the major difference between public sector and private sector banks?

Sneha Sure Sir, public sector banks are those which are operated by government bodies and the employees get salaries from the government funds. Private sector banks on the other hand are the banks which are controlled by the private lenders with the approval from the RBI. Their interest rates are slightly costly as compared to public sector banks.

Chairman What is fiscal policy, Miss Sneha?

Sneha Sir, fiscal policy refers to the policies framed by the government in order to regulate taxation and for allocation of budgets to various departments for their functioning. From paying the income tax to our demand for better roads and infrastructure everything is affected by the government's fiscal policies.

Member 2 When and why Industrial Development Bank of India (IDBI) was formed?

Sneha Sir, the IDBI, was set-up on 1st July, 1964, to coordinate the activities of other financial institutions, to supplement their resources, to plan and promote industries of key significance to the industrial structure. As an apex financial institution, the IDBI has been assigned special role for planning, promoting and developing industries to fill vital gaps in the industrial structure, providing technical and administrative assistance for promotion, management and expansion of industry and undertaking market and investment research and surveys as also techno-economic studies in connection with development of industries.

Chairman Miss Sneha you must have heard about 'Mudra Bank'. What is its objective? Are there any flaws in it?

Sneha Sir, Mudra stands for Micro Units Development and Refinance Agency Ltd., is a financial institution set up by Government of India. The purpose of Mudra is to provide funding to the non-corporate small business/entrepreneurs sector through various financial institutions like banks, non-banking financial institutions etc. It has been established for funding the 'unfunded'.

Sir, Mudra loans have some flaws which should be sorted out. First concentrating on small or micro will be a difficult process and several commercial banks are hesitating to lend finance support to small scale industries especially from rural areas. Mudra bank promotes shadow banking often referred to the bank functioning within certain boundaries which sometimes become impediment. Some financing agencies like NABARD or SIDBI which are similar to Mudra bank, are not in good shape, hence a cause of worry to newly started Mudra loans.

Member 2 Sneha one of the European country declared economic emergency, this last year? What is the purpose behind this measure?

Sneha Sir, French Government has declared a state of 'Economic Emergency' on 18th, January 2016. The purpose behind such declaration is to boost French's stagnant growth and reduce chronic unemployment.

Chairman What do you understand by the term 'mixed economy'? What type of economy does India have?

Sneha A mixed economy is a golden mean between a capitalist economy and a socialist economy. It is an economic system where price mechanism and economic planning are used side by side. A mixed economy has a public sector which is under the control and direction of the state. Public utilities such as rail, road building, canals, power supply, means of communication are included in the public sector. There is also private sector where production and distribution of goods and services are done by private enterprises. The sector operates under state regulations in the interest of public welfare and certain sectors of private operation can be farming, mines, internal and external trade and in the manufacturing of consumer goods and some capital goods. The principal aim of a mixed economy is to maximise social welfare. This incorporates the merits of socialism and avoids the demerits of capitalism. It maintains a general balance between the public sector and the private sector. India, has a mixed economy in which government plays a major role as central planner, regulator, investor, manager and producer.

Member 1 Miss Sneha, do you think that public sector has not done well in India. What are the reasons for it?

Sneha Sir, I beg to differ from you on the issue that public sectors in India have not done well. It is difficult to think of the Indian economy without public enterprises in tune with India's socio-economic and demographic reality.

After India's independence, the main thrust was on economic development with social perspective. To achieve this target the process of setting up national champion in strategic sector–like heavy industry, steel, oil and gas, banking and insurance–was initiated. Some of the target and most successful PSUs BHEL, State Bank of India, ONGC, Indian Oil Corporation, Steel Authority of India are doing well even now and have inducted modern technologies to achieve the best results. Performance of public sector units should not be judged by what they earn in the form of profits but by the total additions they make to the flow of goods and services in the economy. Public sector has also done well in providing employment at large scale with better wages and other facilities compared to the private sector.

Member 2 When was IMF created? How does it work?

Sneha At the end of World War II, the IMF was born at Bretton Wood Conference in 1945. It was created out of a need to prevent economic crisis like the Great Depression.

It is a specialised agency of United Nations and is run by its 186 member countries. The IMF is responsible for the creation and maintenance of international monetary system by which international payments among countries take place. It thus strives to provide a systematic mechanism for foreign exchange transactions.

Member 2 Inspite of good economy, India is still considered a developing country, not a developed one. Why?

Sneha Sir, India's rapid economic growth in recent decades has been a matter to cheer but there is a huge failure at the social indicators. Income distribution has been more unequal and rapid, economic growth has not been used to expand the social and physical infrastructure in a well planned way. There is lack of essential social services (from schooling and health care to the provision of safe water and drainage) for a huge part of the population. India has overtaken other countries in generating real income but it been overtaken in terms of social indicators by many of these countries, even within the region of South Asia itself. Take the example of Bangladesh. Though in India per capita income is almost double in comparison to Bangladesh, but Bangladesh has overtaken India in terms of social indicators like life expectancy, child survival, enhanced immunisation rates, reduced fertility rates, etc.

Member 1 What is E-Governance, Miss Sneha?

Sneha Sir, E-Governance is the application of Information and Communication Technology (ICT) for delivering government services, exchange of information communication transactions, various stand alone systems and services between government to customer, government to business etc. Through E-Governance government services will be made available to citizens in a convenient, efficient and transparent manner.

Chairman Miss Sneha some subsidy reforms have been initiated by the present government? How is direct benefit transfer is proving successful?

Sneha Till now subsidy was largely provided 'at source'. In case of fertilisers, foodgrains and kerosene sold through public distribution system, consumers get the commodities at lower market rates. Under direct benefit transfer scheme, the consumer is asked to pay the market price for any particular commodity (LPG or seeds) and the amount is transferred to his bank account, which is the difference between market rates and subsidised rates. The scheme of direct benefit transfer scheme has been very successful as the subsidy has been received by the genuine person. It is hoped that crediting subsidies into the bank accounts will reduce leakages, delays etc. e.g. the subsidy on LPG, cylinders is directly credited to consumers Aadhar linked bank accounts. As soon as they book a subsidised gas cylinder they get an advanced in their bank accounts.

Chairman Miss Sneha do you have any hobby?

Sneha Sir, during my spare time I read books and novels and listen to good old Indian music.

Chairman Classical music or light music.

Sneha Sir, I am fond of light music as it serves as a real stress buster for me. After a day's hardwork, good light music really soothes our nerves.

Member 1 Our interview is over. Do you have any question to ask?

Sneha No Sir, I do not have any question. (Keeps sitting)

Chairman OK, Miss Sneha, you may leave now.

Sneha Thank you Sirs (Gets up quietly and leaves the room without making any sound).

10. SAMPLE INTERVIEW FOR LIC AAO

Anamika Rastogi belongs to Meerut, a town in UP. She has done graduation with economics as one of the subjects. She is dressed in black trousers and white shirt. She is endowed with intellectual ability of a very high order. She has a good command over English language. She is at present employed as an assistant in the Ministry of Home Affairs Government of India, New Delhi. She has come for an interview for the post of an Assistant Administrative Officer in LIC (Life Insurance Corporation of India, New Delhi).

Miss Anamika Rastogi enters the interview room and wishes the chairman and other members of the board.

Chairman Miss Rastogi, please take your seat.

Anamika Thank you Sir, (She takes the seat meant for the candidate).

Chairman Miss Rastogi, you are working. Where are you employed?

Anamika Sir, I am employed in the Ministry of Home Affairs, Government of India.

Member 1 On what post are you working Miss Rastogi?

Anamika Sir, I am working as an Assistant.

Chairman What is the responsibility of administrative division under this Ministry of Home Affairs (MHA)?

Anamika Sir this division is responsible for handling all administrative and vigilance matters, allocation of work among various divisions in the ministry and monitoring of compliance of furnishing information under the Right to Information Act, 2005, matters relating to the table of precedence, Padma Awards, Gallantry Awards, Jeevan Raksha Padak Awards etc.

Member 1 What is Right to Information Act? What is its basic objective?

Anamika Sir, Right to Information (RTI) Act is an Act of the Parliament of India "to provide right to information for citizens of India".

Its objective is to empower the citizens, promote transparency and accountability in the working of the government and make our democracy work for the people in real sense. The Act is a big step towards making the citizens informed about the activities of the government.

Member 1 Can you say that it has been successful so far?

Anamika Sir, overall it has been hugely successful and has helped citizens get crucial information. One of the biggest successes has been getting information in the Adarsh Scam. It also helped in exposing Public Distribution System in Assam.

Chairman Why do you want yourself to shift in insurance sector?

Anamika Sir, though there is security in government jobs but lack of job satisfaction is there. I love challenges in life and I think insurance sector is full of challenges and has more growth opportunities as well.

Member 2 What is a third party insurance?

Anamika An insurance policy that covers the damage caused by another person or party is known as third party insurance. In this type of insurance, the insured is the first party, insurance company is the second party while the damage done by another is referred as the third party.

This type of insurance policy is purchased for the vehicles so that in case of the accidents they can claim it.

Chairman If you are selected, you will be required to work as a part of a team? How comfortable you are working in a team, Miss Anamika?

Anamika Sir teamwork is required even in government sector. We have to work in a coordinated manner. I am very comfortable working as a part of team.

Chairman What is MODVAT, Miss Rastogi?

Anamika MODVAT refers to an Excise Duty Scheme introduced in 1986 for allowing relief to final manufacturers on the excise duty borne by the suppliers for goods manufactured by them. It has now been replaced by the CENVAT scheme.

It applies to certain specific items and is meant to limit the cascading effect of duty incidence on a number of goods where the MODVAT credit can be claimed on the purchase of raw materials on which excise has been paid.

This MODVAT credit can be used to set off the excise duty payable on subsequent manufacture of goods.

Member 2 Who can buy a insurance policy?

Anamika To buy a insurance policy the conditions are

- Any person who has attained majority and is eligible to enter into a valid contract can insure himself/herself and those in whom he/she has insurable interest.
- Policies can also be taken, subject to certain conditions, on the life of one's spouse or children.
- While underwriting proposals, certain factors such as the policyholder's state of health, the proponent's income and other relevant factors are considered by the Corporation.

Member 2 What are the Objectives of LIC?

Anamika Objectives of LIC are

- Spread and provide life insurance to the masses at a reasonable cost.
- Maximise mobilisation of people's savings by making insurance-linked savings adequately attractive.
- Meet the various life insurance needs of the community that would arise in the changing social and economic environment, etc.

Member 1 When did the LIC of India come into existence?

Anamika In 1956, LIC of India came into existence.

Member 2 What is Foreign Direct Investment (FDI) limit in Insurance Sector?

Anamika Previously FDI limit in Insurance Sector was 26% but now it has been increased to 49%.

Member 2 What is the difference between marketing and sales?

Anamika Marketing and sales are important aspects in business. Both are inevitable activities in any organisation.

Difference between marketing and sales include

- Marketing is considered to be a wider term than sales. It includes identifying customers, producing innovative products, branding, advertising, public relations, sales, etc. Thus, sales is just a stage or an activity of marketing.
- Marketing is the process of creating demand for a product in the market whereas sales refers to fulfilling these demands.
- Marketing helps the organisation to create a brand image of the product or service in the minds of the people while sales involves the selling of that product or service.

Member 1 Where is corporate office/headquarters of LIC located?

Anamika Its corporate office is located in Mumbai.

Chairman How technology was used in general elections in India in 2014?

Anamika Sir, the Election Commission used Electronic Voting Machines (EVM) in the elections. It also launched a website in 1998 which provides accurate information, management administration and instant results of the elections. Use of photo Id cards and computerisation of electoral rolls are all due to use of technology in elections.

Political parties and leaders also used web conferencing, Facebook and Twitter accounts and Google for election purposes.

Member 1 Who made the layout of Delhi?

Anamika Sir, it was Sir Edwin Lutyens and Sir Herbert Baker.

Member 2 What do you mean by NYSE?

Anamika Sir, its New York Stock Exchange and it is situated in 11, Wall Street, Manhattan in New York.

Chairman Miss Anamika, do you pursue any hobby?

Anamika Sir, I hardly get time to pursue a hobby but I read newspaper everyday. Sometimes if I get time, I like to read some magazines also. I am fond of travelling and visiting places full of natural beauty.

Chairman Do you have any question to ask or should we call it a day?

Anamika No, Sir, I don't have any question.

Chairman You may leave now Miss Rastogi.

Anamika Thank you Sirs, (She wishes the chairman and the other members of the board and leaves the interview room).

11. SAMPLE INTERVIEW FOR LIC AAO

Mani Iyer is graduate in Economics. He has dressed himself for the occasion in light blue shirt and navy blue trousers with a matching stripped tie. He walks with careful and confident steps, displaying resoluteness, determination and eagerness. He reaches the interview venue well before the scheduled time and completes various formalities concerning the interview. He was talking to the other candidates in the waiting room when a messenger summons him for the interview. He proceeds briskly towards the interview room, walking with firms steps. He taps the door gently and enters the room. He does not forget to close the door behind him.

Mani Good morning to you all, Sirs.

Chairman Good morning Mani. Please take your seat and feel comfortable.

Mani Thank you very much Sir (He occupies the seat without making any unnecessary movement and noise).

Chairman You have mentioned in your bio-data that your hobbies are watching Hindi movies and eating North Indian cuisines. It is quite surprising that despite being a South Indian, you like Hindi movies and North Indian cuisines.

Mani Iyer Sir I was born and brought up in Delhi. My father who owns a business of electronic goods has settled in Delhi. Therefore, I have seen North Indian culture around me–Hindi movies, North Indian goodies like chats and paranthas, etc.

Member OK, you were born in Delhi. Do you know which is world's tallest brick minaret situated in Delhi? Who had constructed it?

Mani The Qutab Minar is the world's tallest brick minaret at 72.5 metres. It was built by Qutub-ud-din-Aibak of Slave dynasty in 1192.

Chairman What do you know about life insurance?

Mani Life insurance is a contract between the policy owner and the insurer, where the insurer agrees to reimburse the occurrence of the insured individual's death or other event such as terminal illness or critical illness. The insured agrees to pay the cost in terms of insurance premium for the service. The contract is valid for payment of the insured amount during

- The date of maturity
- Specified dates at periodic intervals
- Unfortunate death, if it occurs earlier.

Chairman Why is it important to get life insurance?

Mani Sir, to get life insurance is important because of various reasons like

- This insurance is ideal for people who wish to make the necessary arrangements to guarantee the wellness of their loved beings after their death.
- It will assist you financially if you suffer a serious illness or injury as well as help your loved ones financially if you die.
- It also lowers the cost to the taxpayer in having to support families of people who have become seriously ill, injured or who have died.

Member How do you look at the growth of insurance sector in India?

Mani Insurance is one of the biggest sectors in Indian economy. This sector employs more than 2 lakh people as officers and operational cadre. This sector provides immense employability and growth prospect to those having technical qualification such as PGDM (Insurance).

Member When did insurance business start in India?

Mani In 1818, Oriental Life Insurance Company was opened in Kolkata. It was the beginning of insurance business in India.

Chairman When did Life Insurance Corporation come into existence and why?

Mani Sir, on 19th January, 1956 an ordinance was issued, nationalising the life insurance sector and Life Insurance Corporation came into existence in this year only. The reason for nationalising life insurance sector was due to existence of too many small Indian and foreign private companies and competition was very high. There were allegation of unfair trade practises. The Government of India there started Life Insurance Corporation which absorbed 154 Indian and 16 non-Indian insurance companies.

Member Mr. Mani, after nationalising the insurance sector, why Indian government has allowed private sector to operate in India?

Mani Sir the insurance sector is a colossal one and is growing at a rate of 15-20%. The main objective of allowing private players was to increase competition and enhance customer satisfaction through increased customer choice and lower premiums but ensuring the financial security of the market. To regulate the insurance sector both government and private insurance companies, the IRDA (Insurance Regulatory and Development Authority) was constituted as an autonomous body.

Chairman What are the key objectives of IRDA?

Mani Some of the key objectives of IRDA are

- Issuing a certificate of registration to the applicant as well as modify, renew, withdraw, suspend or cancel any such registration that is deemed unfit.
- Promotion of efficiency in the conduct of insurance business.
- Specifying requisite qualifications, practical training and code of conduct for insurance intermediaries, insurance brokers and agents, etc.

Member What are the different types of insurance available?

Mani Sir, actually there are two main types of insurance, namely life insurance and general insurance which covers different aspect in our life.

Chairman How is general insurance different from life insurance?

Mani Sir, life insurance is a protection against pre-mature death of a person. General insurance refers to insurance for anything other than life. It covers loss of a property, expenses for medical treatment, car insurance, etc.

Chairman What is the role of Development Officer?

Mani Role of Development Officer include

- To guide, supervise and direct the activities of the agents placed under your supervision by the Corporation.
- To introduce suitable persons to the Corporation for appointment as new agents.
- To act generally in such a way as to activate existing agents and motivate new agents, so as to develop a stable agency force.

Chairman What is the difference between life assurance and life insurance?

Mani Life insurance, insures you for a specific period of time. Then if you die at the same time as the policy is in force, the insurance company pays the claim. However, if you survive to the end of the term, the policy is finished and has no lasting value whatsoever. Even at the same time as the life insurance policy is in force it only has any value if you have a claim- in that context it's just like your home insurance. Life insurance is much cheaper than life assurance and in our experience, life insurance is what most people need.

While, a life assurance policy joins a guaranteed insured sum with a none guaranteed investment, the value of the investment being directly related to the size of the guaranteed sum on your policy, the number of years the policy has been in force and Insurance Company's investment performance.

If you were to die during a life assurance policy's term, the policy pays out the guaranteed sum (just as with life insurance) or the value of the annual investment bonuses that had been added to the policy by the insurance company to date, whichever is the larger.

Chairman In India, while casting her vote in any election, what type or right does a women exercise?

Mani Sir, it is the political right of any women to caste vote in the election.

Member If a Vice-President is to be removed from his office, what procedure is to be adopted?

Mani Sir, a resolution is initiated in the Rajya Sabha for the removal of Vice-President. If the resolution is passed with more than 50% of effective membership and agreed to by a simple majority of the Lok Sabha members, the Vice-President can be removed from his office.

Member OK. Mr. Mani, your interview is over. You may leave now.

Mani Thank you Sirs. (He wishes the chairman and other members and gently leaves the interview room).

12. SAMPLE INTERVIEW FOR INTELLIGENCE BUREAU ACIO GRADE-II

Devansh Tyagi is a postgraduate in Political Science from Meerut University securing 78% marks. He is tall, slim and healthy. He has dressed himself appropriately and carefully for the formal occasion. This indicates that he is taking the interview earnestly and that he is determined to achieve success in the interview. He is able to cultivate friendship and get along harmoniously with other people. When he is called for the interview he walks confidently and enters the interview room after taking permission from the board-members.

Devansh Good morning to you all Sirs.

Chairman Good morning, Mr. Devansh. Please be seated and feel comfortable.

Devansh Thank you very much Sir (He occupies his seat gracefully without making any noise).

Chairman Well, your name is quite fascinating. What is the meaning of your first name Mr. Tyagi?

Devansh Sir Devansh means divine or a divine messenger.

Chairman Why do you want to join IB?

Devansh I want to do something challenging and motivating.

Member 1 OK Devansh what is intelligence according to you?

Devansh Sir, it is an ability to acquire and apply knowledge and skills.

Member 2 What is counter-intelligence?

Devansh Sir, it is an intelligence service charged with keeping sensitive information from an enemy, deceiving the enemy, preventing sabotage and collecting political and military information.

Chairman Do you know the difference between IB and RAW.

Devansh Sir, RAW or Research and Analysis Wing, is India's external intelligence agency, works directly under, PMO, but reports to Indian National Security Advisor. It protects nation's interest in annonymity. Sir Intelligence Bureau or IB is India's internal intelligence agency which works under Ministry of Home Affairs (MHA). It primarily deals with counter terrorism, naxal insurgency, etc.

Member 1 What do you understand by the word 'crime'?

Devansh	Sir, a crime is an unlawful act punishable by a state or other authority.
Member 1	Where the headquarters of IB located and it works under which ministry?
Devansh	Sir, headquarters of IB is located in New Delhi and it works under the Ministry of Home Affairs.
Chairman	To which parties do Obama, Bush and Clinton belong?
Devansh	Sir, Barack Obama and Clinton belong to Democratic Party whereas George W Bush belonged to Republican Party of America.
Member 1	OK, Devansh what is the other name of Chanakya. What are his views on state?
Devansh	Chanakya is also known by the name 'Kautilya.' According to Chanakya, a state should have seven organs to work properly. They are Master or King, Ministers, Janpada or Country, Fort, Treasury, Punishments and Friends.
Chairman	What are 6 fundamental rights of a citizen in India?
Devansh	Sir, the 6 fundamental rights are Right to Equality, Right to Freedom, Right against Exploitation, Right to Freedom of Religion, Right to Cultural Expression and Education and Right to Constitutional Remedies.
Member 2	How many schedules are there in the Indian Constitution?
Devansh	Sir, at present Indian Constitution has 12 schedules.
Member 2	What does it imply when we say India is a 'secular' state?
Devansh	It implies that India is non-partisan in its relations with citizens, no matter what religion they belong to. It also implies that the state will not identify with any religion or be influenced by it. No one will be discriminated in the eyes of the laws on the basis of religion.
Chairman	Can you tell us difference between terrorism and insurgency?
Devansh	Yes Sir, terrorism is the calculated use of unlawful violence or threat to inculcate fear, intended to coerce or to intimidate governments or societies in the pursuit of goals that are generally political or religious. Insurgency on the other hand is a movement or a political effort with a specific aim and requires the active or tacit support of some portion of the population involved.

Member 1 Well, Devansh do you have any hobbies?

Devansh I am fond of reading and listening to music.

Member 1 What type of music classical or light music?

Devansh Sir I listen to light music as it is a great way to destress myself. I feel totally relaxed after listening to music for half an hour.

Chairman Do you have any question, you may ask us?

Devansh No, Sir, thank you very much, I do not have any question.

Chairman You may leave now.

Devansh Thank you Sirs (He wishes the chairman and other members leaves the interview room quietly).

13. SAMPLE INTERVIEW FOR INTELLIGENCE BUREAU JUNIOR ENGINEER

Mr Amulya Charan is a B.Sc honours graduate from Manipal, Karnataka and has done electrical engineering from Ranchi Engineering college. He is young, cheerful, confident and mixes well with other candidates. He has dressed himself in white shirt and black trousers with grey tie. After making all the formalities at the reception centre, he went to the waiting hall. After a few minutes, his name is called for the interview. He procceds towards his interview room and before entering, he generally knocks at the door to seek formal permission of the interview board members. He walks in and goes towards the Chairman and other members of the board who are sitting behind a big table.

Amulya Good Morning to you all, Sirs.

Chairman Good morning, Mr Amulya, please be seated (He indicates the chair reserved for the candidate).

Amulya Thank you Sir (He occupies the chair smartly, waiting for a question from the panel).

Chairman Mr Amulya after doing gaduation, you have done electrical engineering also. Why do you want to join IB then? With your qualification you may get lucrative job in private companies also.

Amulya Sir, I know I can get a good job in private companies, but I have a fascination for IB from childhood. My elder brother is in Indian Air Force. I also want to serve my nation but through another medium that is IB.

Member 1 You have done your schooling and graduation from Manipal, Karnataka. Tell me Mr Amulya which city in India is ranked on top in Swachh Bharat Ranking?

Amulya Sir, it is city of Mysuru in Karnataka.

Chairman Mr Amulya, some researchers from Osmania University in Hyderabad spotted a new species of Gecko, a type of lizard usually found in warm climates in which part of India?

Amulya Sir it was spotted in group of Monuments at Hampi, Karnataka.

Member 1 Mr Amulya Charan, you have done your electrical engineering. Can you tell us how tansformer works?

Amulya Sir, transformer is an electrical device that transfers energy between two or more circuits through electromagnetic induction. Transformer is the means through which high voltage electricity from power plants to the lower voltage electricity is used by factories, offices and homes.

Chairman Mr Amulya, if a DC series motor is started on very light load or no load, what will be the repercussions?

Amulya Sir, it will run at dangerously high speed which may damage the motor mechanically.

Member 2 What is a crowbar?

Amulya Sir, a crowbar is a circuit which is used to protect a voltage sensitive load from excessive DC power supply output voltages.

Chairman Mr. Amulya, what are the internal security threats India is facing?

Amulya Sir it is militancy at some places, religious fundamentalism, cyber insecurity and terrorism are some of the security issues India is facing at present.

Member 1 Mr Amulya, what role does IB plays in public service?

Amulya The chief responsibility of Intelligence Bureau of India is to garner intelligence from within the country and also carry out counter intelligence and counter terrorism tasks. The Intelligence Bureau activities are highly confidential and no publications other than the internal ones do reveal their workings. Their largely speculative task includes clearance of licence to amateur radio professionals. The IB is responsible for granting the basic safety clearances to Indian diplomats and judges before their national oath. On exceptional occasions, Intelligence Bureau Officers interact with the media during acute national crisis.

Member 1 What is the difference between emotional intelligence and intellectual intelligence?

Amulya Sir emotional intelligence is described as a person's ability to manage his feelings so that these feelings are expressed appropriately and effectively. Intellectual intelligence is defined as general cognitive problem solving skills. A mental ability involved in reasoning, perceiving relationships and analogies, calculating learning quickly.

Member 2 Is there any difference between information and intelligence?

Amulya Sir, there is a difference between information and intelligence. The principle difference is that information is merely a data. Data by itself doesn't include any context. But intelligence is cognitive problem solving skills. There is reasoning and analysing ability included in this.

Chairman Mr. Amulya, who is the present President of USA? To which party does he belong?

Amulya Sir Mr. Donald Trump has been elected as the President of USA on 9th November, 2016. He belongs to the Republican Party and it is one of the two biggest political parties in the United States of America.

Member 1 Why did India not participate in SAARC Summit which was held in Islamabad?

Amulya Sir, Indian Government cancelled its participation in SAARC Summit due to increasing cross-border terrorist attacks in the region and growing interference in the internal affairs of member states.

Member Which post is seniormost in IB and who is currently positioned on this post?

Amulya Sir, DIB i.e. the Director of Intelligence Bureau is the seniormost post in IB. Senior IPS Officer is appointed for the same post. Mr. Rajiv Jain is the current directer of IB holding this position from 1st January 2017.

Chairman Mr. Amulya do you have any hobbies?

Amulya Sir, whatever spare time I get, I indulge in sports activities. I love playing football and watching all football matches on the TV.

Member 2 Who is your favourite football player around the globe?

Amulya Sir, he is Cristiano Ronaldo a Portuguese football professional. He plays at a forward position and serves as captain for Portugal. In 2015, Ronaldo had scored his 500th senior career goal for club and country.

Member 2 OK. Mr. Amulya, your interview is over. If you have any question to ask, do not hesitate.

Amulya Thank you very much Sir. I do not have any questions.

Chairman You may leave now.

Amulya Thank you very much Sirs. (He wishes all the members of the board and makes smart exit).

14. SAMPLE INTERVIEW FOR RRB JUNIOR ENGINEER

Ankit Chandra is a young man of average height and medium build. He has done B.Sc honours from Lucknow University. He had cleared the written exam conducted by RRB and has come for an interview for Junior Engineer post. He is dressed in formal shirt and trousers with a striped tie. He walks with careful and confident steps, displaying resoluteness, determination and eagerness. When he is summoned for interview he proceeds briskly towards the interview room, walking with firm steps. He taps the door gently and enters the room after closing the door behind him.

Ankit Good Morning to you all, Sirs.

Chairman Good Morning Mr. Ankit. Please take your seat.

Ankit Thank you very much Sir (He occupies the seat without making any unnecessary movement and noise).

Chairman Where have you come from?

Ankit Sir I have come from Malihabad, Lucknow.

Chairman Mr. Ankit, why Malihabad is famous?

Ankit It is famous for different varieties of mangoes which are grown there, among which Dussheri is the most popular variety. Besides Dussehri, other varieties of mangoes such as Chausa, Fazli, Lucknowa, Safeda, etc are also grown here.

Chairman Mr. Ankit how will you describe yourself?

Ankit Sir, I am an efficient and well-organised person. I enjoy trouble shooting issues and try to come up with the best possible solutions in a timely manner.

Chairman According to your bio-data, Ankit you have done B.Sc hons in Physics. Can you tell us the difference between reflection and refraction of light?

Ankit Yes Sir, when a ray of light comes back from hitting a surface, this phenomenon is known as reflection of light. Whereas when a ray of light passes through from one medium to another, it deviates either towards or away from the normal. This phenomenon is called the refraction of light.

Member 1 Mr. Chandra had you ever heard about the term neutral buoyancy? If yes, what does it mean?

Ankit Sir neutral buoyancy is the net upward force experienced by an object submersed in a fluid. Pascal's principle dictates that fluid pressure on an object increases with depth so there is greater pressure on the bottom of the object than the top, resulting in a net upward force.

Chairman What do you know about 'Rail Tel?'

Ankit Sir, Rail Tel Corporation, a PSU, is one of the largest neutral telecom infrastructure provider in the country owning a pan India optic fiber network on exclusive right of way along railway track. Rail Tel with strong nationwide presence is committed to bring cutting edge technology and offers innovative services to the Indian telecom market.

Member 1 What are the required components to design a cross over between parallel tracks?

Ankit Sir the components required to design a cross over between parallel tracks are two switch points, two acute angle crossing and four check rails.

Member 2 In which rail region did the automatic signal system start?

Ankit Sir, it was started in Central Railway.

Member 2 Which is the only railway station that has all three rails in operation?

Ankit Sir it is Dumdum Railway Station. It operates EMU Rail Service, Circular Railway and Metro Rail all three side by side.

Chairman Which company manufactured first indigenous rail compartment and when?

Ankit Sir ICF manufactured first indigenous rail compartment on 2nd October, 1955.

Member 1 Which Indian state has maximum rail routes?

Ankit Sir Uttar Pradesh has maximum rail routes.

Chairman What is 'isolation' in connection with the Indian Rails?

Ankit Sir, 'isolation' refers to method of protecting one line from the adjacent lines. e.g. in the case of loop lines that branch out from the main line at a station.

A train or any rolling stock that is stopped on one of the lines while another train is moving through on the adjacent line should be prevented from moving and running over the points to the main line.

Member 1 Before independence Asif Ali was the Rail Minister. Who was the first Rail Minister after independence?

Ankit Sir Dr John Mathai was the first Rail Minister after independence.

Chairman Which is the longest train in India?

Ankit Sir this is Prayagraj Express which runs between New Delhi to Allahabad. It has 26 coaches.

Member 2 Mr Ankit which Railway is also known as 'Blue Chip' of the Indian Railway?

Ankit Sir, South-Eastern Railway has come to play a strategic role in the nation's industrial and developmental activities and is aptly called 'Blue Chip' of the Indian Railways.

Chairman Well, Mr Ankit, are you interested in sports or do you pursue any hobby?

Ankit Sir, I play hockey, whenever I get time.

Member 1 What is India's achievement in the field of hockey recently?

Ankit Sir, India's hockey team has won Asian Champions Trophy by beating Pakistan by three goals to two.

Chairman Mr Ankit, your interview is over. Would you like to ask any question?

Ankit No Sir, Thank you very much.

Member 2 You may leave now.

Ankit Thank you Sirs, (Gets up and leaves the room without making any noise).

15. SAMPLE INTERVIEW FOR RRB ASSTT. STATION MASTER

Rajiv Arora has done B.Sc Honours in Physics from Delhi University. He is well dressed in formal clothes for the interview. His smiling face and friendly manners exude confidence and warmth. In the waiting hall, he is relaxed with pleasant smile. He easily succeeds in creating a favourable impact on other candidates. When he is called for the interview, he walks confidently towards the interview room. He enters the room after taking permission from the board members and greets the members of the board.

Rajiv Good Morning to you all Sirs.

Chairman Good Morning Mr Rajiv, please take your seat (He indicates the chair meant for the candidate).

Rajiv Thank you very much Sir (He occupies the chair smartly).

Chairman Mr. Rajiv tell me something about yourself.

Rajiv Sir, I belong to Delhi. My schooling is from CBSE Board and I have done B.Sc (Hons) in Physics from Delhi University.

Member 1 Mr. Rajiv what do you understand by RRB?

Rajiv Sir, RRB is Railway Recuitment Board which works under the Government of India. There are 21 boards situated in different parts of country. It provides opportunities to work at different posts in the Indian Railways.

Member 1 Which is the biggest rail zone in terms of network?

Rajiv Sir, Northern Railway is one of the nine old zones of Indian Railways and also the biggest in terms of network having 6807 km route. It covers many states including Jammu and Kashmir, Punjab, Haryana, Himachal Pradesh, Uttarakhand, Uttar Pradesh and Union Territory of Delhi and Chandigarh. It's headquarters is Baroda House, Parliament Street, New Delhi.

Member 2 Mr Rajiv, who was the first female to become the member of Railway Board?

Rajiv Sir, Miss Vijaylakshmi Viswanathan is the first female to be inducted into the Railway Board. She was working as additional General Manager, Southern Railway. She will be the incharge of budgeting and will assist the Financial Commissioner of the Railways.

Chairman Mr Rajiv do you know which is the longest railway bridge of Indian Railways?

Rajiv Yes Sir, Vembanad rail bridge in Kerala is the longest rail bridge in India. With a total length of 4.62 km. It is dedicated solely for freight. The bridge is built over the Vembanad lake and passes through three small islands.

Chairman Mr Rajiv who was first female Asstt. Station Master in Indian Railway?

Rajiv Sir, Miss Rinku Sinha was the first female Asstt. Station Master, who was appointed in 1994 in Eastern Railway, Kolkata.

Member 2 Indian Railways has two heritage hotels. Can you tell us where they are located?

Rajiv Yes Sir, first heritage hotel is located in Puri in Odisha and the other one is in Ranchi. Hotel Puri unfurls before a tourist a sense of timeless grace and a truly reminiscent of the bygone era. Hotel Ranchi is set amidst the sylvan settings of the Chota Nagpur plateau. The hotel has 9 AC and 13 non AC rooms, a lounge and a library.

Chairman What is stamp collection called?

Rajiv Philately Sir.

Member 2 Who founded Brahmo Samaj?

Rajiv Raja Rammohan Rai, Sir.

Chairman Mr. Rajiv do you have any hobbies?

Rajiv Sir, during my spare time I read books and newspapers or magazines.

Member 1 Can you tell me Mr. Rajiv who is the author of the book 'Family Life'?

Rajiv Yes, Sir. I recently read this book. Its author is Akhil Sharma who is Indian-born American author.

Chairman It is your first attempt in RRB. What will you do if you are not selected?

Rajiv No Sir, this is my second attempt for RRB. I am hopeful to clear this exam this time.

Chairman Mr Rajiv, do you want to ask us any question?

Rajiv No Sir, no questions from my side.

Member 2 You may leave now.

Rajiv Thank you very much Sirs (He wishes the members of interview board and leaves the room without making any noise).

16. SAMPLE INTERVIEW FOR RAIL CORPORATION CUSTOMER RELATION ASSISTANT

Amit Sanyal is a science graduate and has been called by DMRC for the post of Customer Relation Assistant. He has dressed himself formally for the occasion.

He was sitting in the waiting room, a messenger summons him for the interview. He proceeds briskly towards the interview room walking with firm steps. He taps the door gently and enters the room. He does not create any noise while entering and takes the seat meant for the candidate.

Amit Sanyal Good Morning to you all, Sirs.

Chairman Good Morning Amit. Please take your seat and feel comfortable.

Amit Sanyal Thank you very much Sir. (He occupies the seat without making any unnecessary movement and noise).

Chairman From where did you do your graduation?

Amit Sanyal Sir I had done my graduation from Delhi University.

Chairman Tell me something about Delhi? When did Delhi become a state?

Amit Sanyal Sir, Delhi is the capital of India. It is spread over an area of 1483 square kilometre. In Delhi, one can witness multi-cultural and multi-ethnical system. People of all caste and creed share same platform in this city which makes it a cosmopolitan city. It has an amazing mix of modernisation and carefully presented antiquity. Delhi acquired statehood in 1992.

Chairman Amit Sanyal, what do you understand by DMRC?

Amit Sanyal DMRC is a joint venture company with equity participation from Government of India and Government of National Capital Territory of Delhi. It has been entrusted with the responsibility of implementation of the rail based Mass Rapid Transit System for Delhi, NCR and other metros. It has been certified by United Nations as the first Metro Rail in the world to get carbon credits for reducing greenhouse gas emissions.

Chairman Why do you want to join DMRC?

Amit Sanyal Sir, Delhi Metro is doing a wonderful job by providing ridership to millions of people of all ages and types. I would like to be part of such a system which is providing comfort to large sections of people.

Chairman How can we differentiate between Indian Rail and DMRC?

Amit Sanyal Sir, metro is a mode of transport in metropolitan cities. The word train is usually used to refer to a long distance or an overnight train. A metro runs short distances with more frequent stops. Trains normally run longer distances and transports people to other areas of the country. Metro also runs on elevated platforms (concrete pillared flyover type) and also underground. Trains run only above-ground.

Member Who is the first ethnic Indian women in space?

Amit Sanyal Dr. Kalpana Chawla, an Indian American woman became the first Indian woman to go into space on 19th November, 1997 on a 16 day mission on NASA's Space Shuttle Columbia as a mission specialist.

Member What will be your approach to improve customer service?

Amit Sanyal Sir, Customer Relations Assistant (CRA) performs duty at customer care centre. They are responsible for dealing with commuters, customer services, assisting passengers with disabilities, attending customer grievances, assisting station controller in handling abnormal situations such as crowd management, station evacuation, etc.

Member What do your understand by term customer's satisfaction?

Amit Sanyal Sir, any business depends upon the quality of the service you offer to the customer. To offer this, your need to understand the customer's needs and their problems. Customer satisfaction is a measure of how products and services supplied, meet or surpass customers satisfaction. It has become a key element of business strategy.

Chairman What do you mean by customer service?

Amit Sanyal Customer service is the act of taking care of the customer's need by providing and delivering high quality service and assistance before, during and after the customer's requirements are met.

Chairman OK Mr. Amit Sanyal, the post you have applied for requires professional knowledge of computers. Can you tell us which is the latest version of MS-Word? What is MS Word?

Amit Sanyal Sir, Word-XP is the latest verison of MS-Word. Sir MS-Word is a software which is developed by Microsoft. It is one of the widely used word processing programs.Word processor programs primarily allow users to create and edit text documents.Typical use may include writing an essay or report, creating a resume or writing notes.

Member Mr. Amit Sanyal tell me about a large number of templates that are provided by Microsoft word.

Amit Sanyal Sir, these templates are for generating business documents, they have many built-in formatting features. The user can add his own commands and objects to the existing list.

Chairman OK, Mr. Amit Sanyal. Do you have any hobby or do you play any sports?

Amit Sanyal Sir, I am fond of playing football as well as badminton. I get up early and play football. In the evening, I play badminton for an hour. This routine keeps me fit and energetic.

Member Would you like to ask any question, Mr. Amit Sanyal?

Amit Sanyal No Sir, Thank you very much Sir.

Chairman Mr. Sanyal, you can go now.

Amit Sanyal Thank you Sirs. (He wishes the chairman and member both and leaves the interview room).

17. SAMPLE INTERVIEW FOR BANK CLERK

Mr Nagam Thombu is a 24 year old graduate in Commerce from Arunachal Pradesh University. He has been working for the last 2 years as an Assistant with a private financial consultancy firm located near his home in Assam. He is well dressed in a white shirt and dark suit with tie. When his name is announced, he confidently moves to the open door of the interview room from which the previous interviewee has just come out. Three men are sitting at a large office table in the centre of the room. He gently knocks on the door for getting permission to enter.

Nagam May I come in, Sir?

Member Yes, Mr Thombu. (pointing to the candidate's chair) Please sit down.

Nagam (sitting down) Thank you, Sir. Good morning to all of you.

Member 1 Mr Thombu, you have done very well in the Banking Section of the Common Written Examination (CWE). How did you achieve this?

Nagam (looking around and making eye contact one by one with all three interviewers) Sir, you will be aware from my bio-data that for the last two years I have been working with a private financial consultancy firm in Assam. The proprietor of this firm is arranging business loans from banks for his customers through his contacts in the various banks in our area. He knew the procedures required and what information was acceptable to the banks, as he had been a banker himself earlier and had taken voluntary retirement to start this business. He trained me up to go physically to the banks for getting all the formalities completed for our customers. Thus, I came to know all the banking rules and procedures very well. This knowledge helped me to maximise my score in the Banking Section of the CWE.

Chairman Now that you have brought it up, Mr Thombu, tell us what you found as the most problematical condition for your customers which the banks refused to relax.

Nagam Sir, the most problematical condition for my customers was the provision of collateral. The banks insisted that there should be some immovable asset like a plot of land or a house or building in the name of the person in whose name the loan was to be taken. This immovable asset would then be pledged to the bank for the duration of the loan. This was a form of guarantee to the bank that the loan would be returned with the interest due. (As he pauses, one member of the interview board interrupts.)

Member 1 Now let us understand if you know what your duties are expected to be.

Nagam Certainly, Sir. A bank clerk may be asked to perform a variety of duties, depending on the size of the bank branch he is posted in or if he is posted to other offices of the bank. The most common duties are to receive cash deposits, encashing cheques presented and handling cash withdrawals. To perform such operations, the bank clerk must perform identification checks of customers and ensure validity of signature on cheques and other documents. Other duties can include transferring funds from one account to another, preparing bank drafts, making various entries in the banking software used, dealing with customers and solving their problems.

Member 2 Thank you, Nagam. I feel you have covered the duties adequately. For carrying out these duties, what personal characteristics should a bank clerk possess?

Nagam Sir, the first personal quality is being presentable in both appearance and behaviour. Further, a bank clerk must be responsible, a quick and efficient worker committed to flawless performance. This is most important because customers are easily annoyed by mistakes when it comes to their bank accounts and money transactions.

Chairman Good. Now let us come to some current events. Some time back, the Central Government conducted a demonetisation exercise. Can you very briefly inform us what this was and was it successful in its purpose?

Nagam (thinks for a short time) Yes, Sir. The Central Government demonetised ₹ 1000 and ₹ 500 notes overnight. The main purpose was to stifle the parallel economy in our country and bring more people within the net of income tax. I will say that it was largely successful in its intent and purpose. Of course, the bank clerks and officers had to take the load in exchanging the old currency and more importantly, keeping track of who had deposited it and how much. I remember that my proprietor's business suffered during this period of about 2 months, as the banks were not willing to take up our work during those days. All their staff had been shifted to the massive work relating to demonetisation.

Member 1 Good. Now let us come to your personal details. What personal characteristics distinguish you as a candidate for a banking career?

Nagam Sir, first of all, I like dealing with people and solving their problems. It gives me immense mental satisfaction. I also have a good head for figures, as I can mentally calculate very well. You will notice from my Class XII results that I scored a distinction in Mathematics. Further, I work responsibly and reliably, as my current employer will certify. I have never violated his trust. This quality is essential in a banking career.

Chairman Thank you, Nagam. In case you are selected, we will inform you suitably. Good day. (gets up from the chair and shakes hands with all the committee members).

Nagam Thank you, Sir. Good day. (He turns around and leaves the room with a confident air and shuts the door behind him.)

SAMPLE INTERVIEWS FOR PRIVATE SECTOR

- *For Marketing Representative*
- *For HR Executive*
- *For IT Manager and Coordinator*
- *For Office Executive and Sales Executive*
- *For School Teacher*

Here we are providing some mock interviews for the private sectors. These sample interviews will provide an insight into types of questions asked in such interviews. Questions asked may be job specific or company specific. One must remember that in private sectors that there can be more than one rounds of job interviews and in every round, there may be different levels of questions.

1. SAMPLE INTERVIEW FOR FINANCE MANAGER

Hemant Oberoi belongs to Patiala in Punjab. He has just completed his graduation from Patiala. On arrival for the interview he reports at the reception and completes the necessary formalities. Thereafter he proceeds to the waiting hall, where he meets two other candidates. During the course of the conversation, he displays confidence, leadership quality and good communication skills.

As soon as his turn for the interview is announced he stands up, moves towards the interview room. He walks upto the interview room in a firm, steady manner, obtains permission to enter and goes confidently towards the chair meant for the interviewee.

Hemant Good morning Sirs.

Chairman Good morning, Mr. Hemant. Please take your seat.

Hemant Thank you, very much Sir (He occupies the chair meant for the candidate.)

Chairman Mr. Hemant, you have done your graduation from Patiala which is in Punjab. Can you tell us why Punjab is spelled and called so?

Hemant Yes Sir, actually correct spelling of Punjab is Panjab. Pan means (five) and (ab) means water. It is a land of five rivers, which are the Jhelum, the Chenab, the Ravi, the Sutlej and the Beas. That's why the state is called so.

Member You are from Patiala, can you tell us who founded this city?

Hemant Sir, Patiala state was founded in 1763 by Baba Ala Singh, a Jat Sikh chieftan. He also laid foundation of the Patiala fort known as Qila Mubarak, around which the present city of Patiala is built.

Chairman What are your strengths?

Hemant Sir I am hardworking and due to that I can work for more hours and finish my work within a time frame. Moreover, I am adaptable so I can handle any type of people and situation and also bring out the best from them instead of clashing opinions or situations.

Member What have you learnt from your failures so far?

Hemant Sir, I have learnt to analyse myself and find out my shortcomings. I have worked hard on my shortcomings and tried to improve myself in the future. Moreover, I have learnt never to give up, keep trying and trying till I achieve the desired result.

Chairman Mr. Hemant, why do you want to do MBA in finance as mentioned in your resume? You are already working in a company.

Hemant I always had a keen interest in finance. Even at my current job, I am doing a project for the equity research division of one of the largest banks in UK. I found the concepts of company valuation, P/E ratios and asset- ratios and how they relate to a company's share price really interesting. That experience further increased my inclination towards pursuing finance as a career option and that's the reason I want to pursue an MBA. I would like to join a multi-national bank in their equity research division after my MBA.

Member Mr. Hemant can you please explain what the P/E ratios are and how they are related to the company's stock price?

Hemant Sir, the price-earnings ratio (P/E ratio) is the ratio for valuing a company that measures its current share price relative to its per share earnings.

It shows if the market is over valuing or undervaluing the company. A high P/E ratio may indicate that the stock is over priced. A stock with low P/E ratio may have greater potential for rising P.

Member Can you mention some other ratios? How are they useful to know?

Hemant Yes Sir, they are debt to equity ratio, price to book value ratio, operating-profit margin or ratio, Enterprise Value (EV) ratio the PEG ratio etc. Sir looking at the different ratios gives us an easier way to find out about a company's performance. Ratio analysis helps investors to know how the company has been performing and in comparison to other companies; then zero down on the best investment ratios.

Member What is Financial Information Exchange (FIX) protocol?

Hemant The Financial Information Exchange Protocol is an electronic communications protocol for international real time exchange of information related to securities transactions and markets. Most of the electronic trading is done in financial information exchange, though different exchanges have their own native protocol but most of the broker supports Financial Information Exchange Protocol.

Member Mr. Hemant can you define the term National Income?

Hemant National Income is the sum total of money value of all the final goods and services produced in a country during the period of one year. It is an aggregative measure of the value of all the goods and services produced in agriculture, industry, trade and all the other vocations in an economy calculated without any double counting. In other words, it measures the net value added by various sectors of the economy during one year.

Member What is the difference between sell orders and short sell orders?

Hemant Sell means selling your own securities, short selling means selling securities without owning them. Normally broker lend securities to user.

There are two kinds of short sell i.e. covered short sell and naked short sell. Most of the stock exchange don't allow naked short sell because it is normally abused to take stock price downward.

Member What is naked short sell and what is covered short?

Hemant Naked short is when trader sells one stock which they don't own at that moment. Covered short sell means that trader owns stock which they are shorting.

Member What are the different forms of market and how can we differentiate between them?

Hemant Sir, in market economies, there are a variety of different market systems that exist depending on the industry and the companies within that industry. Some of market systems are perfect competition, monopoly, oligopoly, monopolistic competition and monopsony. It is easy to differentiate between them. e.g. perfect competition is a market system characterised by number of different buyers and sellers. In the classic theoretical definition of perfect competition, there are an infinite number of buyers and sellers.

With so many market players, it is impossible for any one participant to alter the prevailing price in the market. If they attempt to do so, buyers and sellers have infinite alternatives to pursue.

A monopoly is the exact opposite form of market system as perfect competition. In a pure monopoly, there is only one producer of a particular good or service, and generally no reasonable substitute. In such a market system, the monopolist is able to charge whatever price they wish due to the absence of competition, but their overall revenue will be limited by the ability or willingness of customers to pay their price.

Chairman Mr. Hemant do you agree that in small businesses and start ups, there is more scope for professional growth?

Hemant Sir, indeed, small business or start ups can give more experience than any MNC as one can explore different fields. A person can execute his/her wild ideas and see if it actually works in the real world, which he/she may not be able to experience in any big company. It can provide job satisfaction and professional growth if one is willing to take risk and work hard for it.

Member Does doing an MBA qualify anyone to start his/her own venture?

Hemant Sir, no, MBA cannot teach enough, of what a person needs to know to start one's own venture. An entrepreneur has to go through idea validation, market research creating a business projection plan, marketing plan, secure funding, launching of product or service and much more. MBA learning may help a person to get a better idea of what to expect and how to react to certain issues but one has to learn himself what is the best way to run his/her business.

Chairman OK Mr Hemant, if you encounter a significant problem with a system, process or procedure, how will you solve it?

Hemant Sir, the system, process or procedure has to be seen in a broader perspective. any problem can be solved with joint efforts only.

Member How would you handle a situation with tight deadliness, Mr. Hemant?

Hemant Sir, so far I have not faced such a problem. But if anytime I am in this situation, I will try to get a clear idea about the project. Planning my work by prioritising the task will certainly help me. Sometime should be given to anticipated or non-anticipated problems. Completing the smaller tasks or activities as planned or scheduled will definitely help me to complete work in a tight schedule or deadlines.

Member According to you, what makes a person good manager?

Hemant Sir, in my views good managers need to be more than just liked by their team members. They have to be efficient, firm when required, keen to do follow up about the status and deadlines and they should ensure to give feed back to the staff so that any short coming can be rectified. They should have a vision and should be able to motivate and inspire their team to do their best. Patient hearing and approachability are some other requirements to be a good manager.

Chairman Do you pursue, any hobby, Mr. Hemant?

Hemant Sir, though I do not get much spare time, but still I own a beautiful garden full of seasonal flowers. I love gardening and I take delight in growing different types of flowers in my garden.

Member Do you have any question to ask from any of us?

Hemant No Sir, I do not have any question.

Chairman You may leave now. Good day.

Hemant Thank you Sirs, good day to all of you Sirs (Leaves the interview room confidently but quietly).

2. SAMPLE INTERVIEW FOR IT MANAGER

Vikas Shetty has completed his MCA from Delhi University. He bears a friendly and optimistic outlook confidence. He walks confidently towards other candidates in the waiting hall and after wishing them, he introduces himself and shakes hand firmly with each one. As soon as his name is called for the interview, he walks briskly towards the interview room and seeks a formal permission to enter the room. On being allowed, he moves towards the chair meant for the candidate.

Vikas Good Morning, Sir.

Chairman Good Morning, Mr. Vikas, please take your seat and be comfortable. (He indicates towards the chair).

Vikas Thank you very much Sir, (He occupies the chair without making much noise and movement).

Chairman How far the computer knowledge is useful for a candidate, who seek a job in any organisation irrespective of type and class of a job?

Vikas In today's technologically oriented economy, it is no surprise that a person with strong computer skills fare better in the job market than their technically challenged counterparts. This trend influences virtually all jobs, not just technology-centered positions.

Member What is 'Digital India Programme'? Are you aware of it?

Vikas Yes Sir, Digital India is a campaign launched by the Government of India to ensure that government services are made available to citizens electronically by improving online infrastructure and by increasing internet connectivity or by making the country digitally empowered in the field of technology.

Member Do you remember the 'tag line' given to this programme.

Vikas Sir, I think it is 'Power to Empower'.

Chairman Mr Vikas in a country like India, where poverty and unemployment is the big problem, is such a programme justified?

Vikas Sir, initiatives like Digital India can in the long run help to alleviate poverty and unemployment.

Poverty alleviation is an incremental process that needs modern approach, usage of technology, entrepreneurship and public private partnership. Technology will add into the efforts of poverty alleviation. e.g. this initiative will transform a life of a farmer when he comes to know about prevalent prices of his crop at a click of a button in his mobile or either through community data centres being envisaged through Digital India. This new scheme will augment new job opportunities also to our unemployed youths.

Member Can you differentiate computer software and computer program?

Vikas Sir, a computer program is a piece of programming code which performs a well defined task whereas software includes programming code, its documentation and user guide.

Chairman What is Software Development Life Cycle (SDLC)?

Vikas Software development life cycle or software process is the systematic development of software by following every stage in the development process namely requirement gathering, system analysis, design, coding, testing, maintenance and documentation in that order.

Chairman OK Mr Vikas what is object oriented approach in information systems?

Vikas Sir, the object oriented approach to information systems development describes activities as a collection of processes, that interact with data entities, processes, that accept inputs and produce outputs.

Chairman What is six sigma in software technology?

Vikas Sir, six sigma is a statistical measure of variation in a process. It is a problem-solving methodology that can be applied to a process to eliminate the root cause of defects and cost associated with it.

Member Can you define 'tailoring' in software?

Vikas Yes Sir, as the name suggests tailoring is nothing but changing an action to achieve an objective according to conditions. Whenever tailoring is done there should be adequate reasons for it. Even if tailoring is applied, a process should not be by passed or omitted.

Chairman What is configuration management?

Vikas Configuration management is the detailed recording and updating of information for hardware and software components. When we say components we not only mean source code. It can be tracking of changes for software documents such as requirement, design, test cases, etc. The main intention of configuration management is to track our changes if we have issues with the current system. Configuration management is done using baselines.

Member Mr Vikas what is the difference between a defect and a failure?

Vikas Sir, when a defect reaches the end customer it is called a failure and if the defect is detected internally and resolved it is called a defect.

Chairman What does Software Project Manager do?

Vikas Sir, Software Project Manager is engaged with software management activities. He is responsible for project planning, monitoring the progress, communication among stakeholders, managing risks and resources, smooth execution of development and delivering the project within time, cost and quality constraints.

Member Mention some project management tools.

Vikas There are various project management tools used as per the requirement of software project and organisation policies. They include Gantt chart, PERT chart, Resource Histogram, Critical Path Analysis, Status Reports, Milestones Checklist etc.

Member Mr Shetty what challenges are you looking for in this job?

Vikas Sir, I would like to be able to effectively utilise my skills and experience. I have always been motivated by challenges and have the ability to meet challenges. I think I have the flexibility and skills necessary to handle a challenging job.

Chairman What is your biggest weakness?

Vikas Nothing big Sir, but I am still somewhat nervous and uncomfortable with my public speaking skills and I would like to give more presentation and talk infront of others or in meetings.

Member Assuming that you are selected what will be your strategy for next 60 days?

Vikas Sir, if I am selected for this post, I will use my initial days in understanding my role carefully in terms of increasing the overall profitability. I shall formulate my strategy to growth in close conjunction with our seniors as well as my team members.

Member Mr. Vikas can you differentiate between confidence and over confidence?

Vikas Confidence for me is being true to oneself, when one is motivated to do anything and everything. Over confidence means under estimating others and showing himself/herself as unique.

Chairman You have mentioned that you are fond of reading. Could you tell us what types of material you like to read?

Vikas Sir, besides reading newspaper I go through Frontline, and Outlook magazines. I also read regularly science journals and technology related material to keep myself updated on this front.

Chairman OK Mr Vikas, it was really nice to talk you. Our management team will contact you soon.

Vikas Thank you very much, Sirs. (He wishes the member of the interview board and leaves the room).

3. SAMPLE INTERVIEW FOR TRAINEE ENGINEER

Miss Seema Choudhary is a young girl 25 years old, who has passed B.Tech in Electronics and Communications from Anna University, Tamil Nadu. She called for personal interview by BHEL. She is formally dressed, confident, energetic and cheerful. When her name called for the interview, she walks confidently towards interview room. She taps gently and takes permission to enter the interview room.

Seema Good morning Sirs

Chairman Good morning, Miss Seema, please take your seat.

Seema Thank you very much Sir. (Occupies a seat meant for the candidate without making any noise).

Chairman OK Miss Seema, how was your journey? I hope you didn't face any difficulty in locating this place.

Seema No Sir, I had enquired about the place and understood the directions. There was no difficulty in reaching this office.

Member 1 Tell me about yourself.

Seema Thank you very much for giving me this golden opportunity. Let me introduce myself. I have a family comprising of four members. My parents and me and my younger sister. My father's name is Manohar Choudhary who is a doctor. My mother Dimple Choudhary is a house wife. My younger sister Reena is studying in XIth standard.

I had completed my B.Tech in Electronics and Communication from Anna University, Tamil Nadu and schooling from Delhi Public School, R.K. Puram, Delhi. During my graduation period, I had done three mainframe projects and successfully completed a training course on the mainframe. I am excellent in planning, analysing, designing and developing. Whatever task I take in my hand, I do with my full passion and concentration and try to complete the task on time.

Member 1 What are your strengths and weaknesses?

Seema Sir, my greatest strength is my positive attitude, even during the critical times.

During my college project, there were times when our ideas were not falling in place and the outcome was negative. I believed in myself, remained positive and kept my team motivated to persist our idea. Finally, we got the desired result. As far as weakness is considered, Sir I am a perfectionist and tend to concentrate too much on one single task to get it to perfection. It makes me using up my time on single task which is meant for other tasks.

Chairman You have done B. Tech in Electronics and Communications, any particular reason to choose this branch of engineering.

Seema Sir, in the context of wide-spreading technologies ruling every aspect, communication has its own role in making people connect together. Moreover, it finds its application in defence, entertainment, education and various other fields. A wide range of opportunities like in nano technology, robotics, high speed automated processor in embedded system and image processors, are available for budding engineers.

Chairman OK, coming to your subject what is communication in technology?

Seema Sir, communication means transferring a signal from the transmitter which passes through a medium then the output is obtained at the receiver or in layman's language transferring of messages from one place to another place is called communication.

Member 2 Can you tell us what are the different types of communications? Explain.

Seema There are two types of communication. This is analog and digital communication.

As a technology, analog is the process of taking an audio or video signal (the human voice) and translating it into electronic pulse. Digital on the other hand is breaking the signal into a binary format where the audio or video data is represented by a series of '1' s and '0' s. Digital signals are immune to noise, quality of transmission and reception is good, components used in digital communication can be produced with high precision and power consumption is also very less when compared with analog signals.

Member 1 Miss Seema what is electronics?

Seema The study and use of electrical devices that operate by controlling the flow of electrons or other electrically charged particles is called electronics.

Chairman What is CDMA?

Seema CDMA stands for Code Division Multiple Access which uses digital format. In CDMA systems several transmissions via the radio interface take place simultaneously on the same frequency bandwidth. User data is combined at the transmitter's side with a code, then transmitted. On air, all transmission get mixed. At the receiver's side, the same code is used as in transmitter's side.

Member 1 Miss Seema, can you explain Bluetooth?

Seema Bluetooth is designed to a personal area network, where participating entities are mobile and requires sporadic communication with other. It is omni-directional i.e.

it does not have line of sight limitation like infrared does. Ericsson started the work on Bluetooth and named it after the Danish King Harold Bluetooth. Bluetooth operates in the 2.4 GHz area of spectrum and provides a range of 10 metres. It offers transfer speeds of around 720 kbps.

NOTE *(After questions asked on subject some HR personnel who are also part of interview board ask different types of questions).*

Chairman Where do you see yourself in next 5 years from now?

Seema As a fresher I am assuming my first 5 years will be a huge learning curve. I want to absorb much of the industry knowledge I would also like to sharpen my technical abilities. In next five years, I see myself playing various roles in the team from a fresher to leading a team.

NOTE *(This question is to know your career aspirations and how long you will be committed to the organisation. If you have a plan to leave the organisation, in a short time, better explain it with reasoning)*

Member 2 Miss Seema, your interview is over. If you have any question, you may ask.

Seema Thank you very much Sir, I don't have any question.

Chairman You may leave now.

Seema Thank you very much Sirs, leaves the room quietly after wishing everyone.

4. SAMPLE INTERVIEW FOR HR COORDINATOR

The job of HR Coordinator is a middle management level supervisory post in the HR Department of many companies. The HR Coordinator must perform various tasks related to the daily operations of a company's Human Resources (HR) department.

Another important duty is supporting all the HR functions like employee training (identifying training needs, arranging training and feeding back outcomes of training), maintenance of personnel-related data (payroll, personal information, leave etc), performance management, performance review of employees and any other related HR functions.

Ms Parul Sinha is a 29 year old MBA in HR from GGS Indraprastha University with a BA (Hons) degree from Delhi University. After passing her MBA, she worked as a Management Trainee in the HR Department of a large IT company, in which she was trained in all sections of HR. After finishing her one year of training, she joined a startup engineering organisation as an HR Executive. Here she has been working for almost 5 years and has overseen the growth of the organisation into a medium sized company.

When her name is announced, she confidently moves to the open door of the interview room from which the previous interviewee has just come out. Parul gently knocks on the door for getting permission to enter.

Parul May I come in, Sir?

Chairman Yes, Ms Sinha. (pointing to the candidate's chair) Please come in and take your seat.

Parul (sitting down) Thank you, Sir. Good afternoon to both of you.

Member Good afternoon, Parul. I am Rajni Seth, Deputy Manger (HR) in this company and this (indicating the Chairman) is Mr Satish Purkayastha, Head of our HR Department. Tell me, why are you interested in this position?

Parul (making eye contact one by one with both interviewers) Madam, I'm always ready to take on responsibility and feel this will come more quickly and often with a large company like yours. It will give me the chance to build closer working relationships with departmental clients and colleagues. I've found through my past work experience that this makes an organisation more effective as well as more satisfying to work in.

Chairman Don't you think that your present employer has given you that opportunity? As you mentioned in your resume, it is a growing company and thus will give you more opportunities to grow.

Parul Sir, the actual fact is that although the company is growing, the growth in business has slowed down and we are no longer recruiting employees even to fill most of the vacancies caused by employees who leave. Our profitability has reduced to almost zero, as mentioned in our last Annual Report. I feel that my career will stagnate if I stay on more in this company.

(As she pauses, Ms Rajni Seth, member, interrupts.)

Member Okay, we get the idea. Now, Parul, quickly give us the highlights of your career so far.

Parul Yes, Madam. After completing my MBA, I joined Ace Software Limited as a Management Trainee in the HR Department. They rotated me in the six sections that the HR there operates in, i.e. Recruitment, Training, Employee Relations,

Compensation and Benefits, Compliance and finally Record keeping. This gave me an overview of each of these functions.

When Ace Software released me after one year as a Management Trainee, I was offered a job as HR Executive in the engineering organisation where I currently work, Popular Engineers Limited. As the organisation had just started and their factory was still under construction, I had an excellent hands-on experience in all HR functions. I felt pride in helping the organisation to grow from the grassroots level.

However, the company growth has tapered off now because newer technology has been developed for the products being manufactured and our company has not invested in the new technology. Also, I feel that my experience has enabled me to now work fairly independently and I can enhance my career prospects by joining a growing organisation like yours. That sums up my career.

Chairman Thank you, Parul. Tell me whether you are currently located in the factory or at the Head Office of your company?

Parul Sir, at present I am at the Head Office and have been there for the last two years, when most of the HR functions were shifted to the Head Office. However, I visit the factory once every week along with our HR Manager to give immediate solutions to problems raised by the HR persons stationed there.

Chairman We understand. It means that even after five years of the factory being established, the factory HR persons require your services regularly. Can you give me one specific instance of problems you sorted out on visiting the factory which were pending?

Parul Yes, Ma'am, it is about performance management, which occurred recently. One workman had acquired a professional technical qualification by attending evening classes, but was not given a promotion because there was no requirement of this qualification in his department. He approached me with his grievance. As recruitment had been centralised at the Head Office, I was aware that there was an urgent requirement of an employee in another department to replace a person in a critical position who had resigned from the company. This vacancy matched the new qualification and work background of the aggrieved worker. I killed two birds with one stone by arranging the worker's transfer to the other department.

Chairman Congratulations, Parul. You are a real problem solver. Now tell us something about your ambition and how you see yourself five years from now if you join our organisation as an HR Coordinator.

Parul Definitely, Sir. I am keen to join a larger organisation like yours because in my current job I do not feel there is any future. The company business is stagnating. I want to join a growing organisation. I feel your company will continue increasing business for many years to come. I have improved my HR skills for five years and now feel that I can make HR more relevant to the company's business interests so that our Directors and investors realise that HR is as important to the company as the other departments.

In five years from now, I would like to reach the top hierarchy in HR in any division of the company. I want to continue solving employee problems so that productivity remains high. I feel I can do this better in an IT company than in an engineering organisation, as the employees here are more mature in their thinking.

Member One last question, Ms Sinha. You have not informed us of your expectations regarding salary. What salary do you expect and how soon can you join?

Parul Sir, in my resume I have mentioned my current salary and CTC (cost-to-company). I will definitely join your organisation if 10% to 15% more is offered to me. Of course, I will expect quite a lot of freedom in solving employee problems within the framework of the company's policies. You have gone through my resume and understood my employment experience. I am sure you will give me work which will keep me creatively engaged. I am sure I will not disappoint you.

Regarding my joining time, I need to give one month's notice to my present employer according to the terms of the appointment letter. I would like to part ways with my employer amicably.

Chairman Thank you, Ms Sinha. In case you are selected, we will inform you suitably. Good day.

Parul (gets up from the chair and shakes hands with both the committee members). Thank you, Sir. Thank you, Madam. Good day.

(She turns around and leaves the room with a confident air and shuts the door behind her.)

5. SAMPLE INTERVIEW FOR OFFICE EXECUTIVE

Office Executive is a generalist post in any type of organisation. The essential duties of a person doing this work will include filing and retrieving information from organisational documents, records and reports. He will also have to draft, scan, copy and mail documents and letters or supervise the assistants carrying out these operations. He may also have to interact with official visitors and answer telephone calls.

Sarthak Dwivedi is a 24 year old graduate in Commerce from a Central University. He has been working for the last 2 years as an Office Assistant in a small consultancy firm located near his home. When his name is announced, he confidently moves to the open door of the interview room from which the previous interviewee has just come out. Three men are sitting in a semicircle at the far end of a large office table in the centre of the room. He gently knocks on the door for getting permission to enter.

Sarthak May I come in, Sir?

Chairman Yes, Mr Dwivedi. (pointing to the candidate's chair) Please come in and take your seat.

Sarthak (sitting down) Thank you, Sir. Good morning to all of you.

Member 1 Mr Dwivedi, tell me about yourself.

Sarthak (looking around and making eye contact one by one with all three interviewers) Sir, I'm Sarthak Dwivedi, a 24 year old graduate in Commerce from the Central University of Punjab in Bathinda. My home town is Etah in Uttar Pradesh. My father works in a nationalised bank and my mother is a housewife. I have been working in a small consultancy firm here for the last 2 years as an Office Assistant, but feel that now I should take on a more responsible job, as I have understood the basic duties to be carried out in an office.

Chairman Good you have brought that up, Mr Dwivedi. Tell me what you expect are the duties to be performed in a branch office of a medium sized engineering company like ours. Also tell me which of these duties you have performed earlier.

Sarthak Sir, first of all, I expect that I will have to file and retrieve organisational documents, records and reports. I have had adequate experience of this in my current job, where

I am now maintaining all the files pertaining to our clients' correspondence. Of course, in the beginning here, I will need to study and understand the filing system in this office. (As he pauses, one member of the interview board interrupts.)

Member 1 What else, Mr Dwivedi? Let's go through the other duties quickly.

Sarthak Yes, Sir. Next, I will have to draft, scan, copy and mail documents and letters, either through e-mail or through courier. Another duty will be to interact on behalf of the company with any visitors, whether they are from the Head Office, other branch offices or our employees in the field. I may also have to deal with and solve problems faced by our customers, as this is a sales office. In this regard, I have experience in personally dealing with clients in my current job with a consultancy organisation.

As many interactions with customers are carried out over the telephone, I expect I will have to do this also. I pride myself on my spoken English, which I have polished by attending a course in English Speaking, as mentioned in my resume. Besides these duties, I will carry out whatever other duties are assigned to me.

Member 2 Thank you, Sarthak. I feel you have covered all the duties adequately. But how can we judge whether you will be able to send e-mails? (indicating the bio-data lying in front of him) You have not mentioned in your resume that you are computer literate.

Sarthak Sorry, Sir, but at present anybody who works in an office must be computer literate; otherwise he will not be able to perform his duties satisfactorily. That is why I did not mention it. However, I have mentioned in my current job description that I am sending and receiving e-mails on behalf of my organisation. I could not have done this without being computer literate. So you may rest assured that I will be able to do so.

Chairman Yes, we understand. Now, let me explain to you the current job for which you are being interviewed. The job entails leading a clerical workforce of up to 8 employees and looking after all the office work of this branch. This requires the qualities of leadership and teamwork to lead a small workforce in accomplishment of all work related to the branch. The incumbent will report to the Give us an instance in your current job or elsewhere in which you have demonstrated leadership or teamwork successfully.

Sarthak (thinks for a short time) Yes, Sir. A few months ago one of the customers of the consultancy firm where I work refused to pay our bills because of some discrepancy in the amount charged for consultancy work. The proprietor of our consultancy formed a team of three of us. i.e. myself (the record keeper), the Accounts Executive (who billed the customer) and the Consultant (the person who actually executed the consultancy work), to sort out this problem. I coordinated the efforts of our team and enabled the Accounts Executive to communicate directly with the Consultant, which brought the discrepancy to light. I accordingly asked the Accounts Executive to correct one faulty bill issued to the customer, which was agreed to by the Consultant. Thus, the problem was sorted out and the customer paid us the revised amount to the satisfaction of all.

Chairman One last question, Mr Dwivedi. Why do you want to join our organisation?

Sarthak Yes, Sir. I am keen to join a larger organisation like yours because in my current job I cannot progress any further. I am reporting directly to the proprietor there. The consultancy firm's business has not grown during the last two years and it appears that the proprietor is happy with the way his business is going. I have been reading about the progress of your company in the press and have also visited your company's website. I find that the company's business is expanding and it has a bright future. In a few years from now, I would like to head a branch office like this one or specialise in a particular function at the Head Office or elsewhere. It will enable me to use my talent for giving good results to the company.

Chairman Thank you, Sarthak. In case you are selected, we will inform you suitably. Good day.

Sarthak (gets up from the chair and shakes hands with all the committee members). Thank you, Sir. Good day.

(He turns around and leaves the room with a confident air and shuts the door behind him.)

6. SAMPLE INTERVIEW FOR MARKETING REPRESENTATIVE

Marketing Representative is the lowest level post in any type of marketing organisation or in the Marketing Department of a company. The essential duties of a person doing this work will include executing marketing campaigns with the goal of increasing product awareness and increasing sales and profits. Such people are generally required to travel extensively to meet dealers and other customers to generate leads and get orders for supply of goods or services. In many cases they may also have to carry out the functions of a salesman. Kulwant Sareen is a 23 year old graduate in Science from a Central University. He has been working for the last 3 years as a Sales Assistant with a distributor selling construction material to various dealers who supply construction contractors building houses in towns and cities. Now he has been called for interview by a cement manufacturer who supplies various grades of cement to its dealers and distributors.

When his name is announced, he confidently moves to the open door of the interview room from which the previous interviewee has just come out. Two men and a woman are sitting at the far end of a large office table in the centre of the room. He gently knocks on the door for getting permission to enter.

Kulwant (addressing the person in the centre) May I come in, Sir?

Chairman Yes, Mr Sareen. (pointing to the candidate's chair) Please come in and take your seat.

Kulwant (sitting down) Thank you, Sir. Good morning to all of you.

Member 1 Mr Sareen, tell me something about your family background, qualifications, work experience and why you applied for this job.

Kulwant (looking around and making eye contact one by one with all three interviewers) Sir, I am Kulwant Sareen, a 23 year old graduate in Science from the Central University of Haryana in Mahendragarh. My home town is Jind in Haryana. Both my parents work as government teachers in Haryana. I have been working with a distributor of construction materials here for the last 1 years as a Sales Assistant, travelling to various dealers, collecting orders from them and arranging deliveries. Of course, I also ensure timely payment against deliveries. However, the distributor I work with is a proprietorship firm and not well-organised. Now I feel that I have gained some knowledge in this field. So I am looking for better long-term career prospects in an organised company like yours. That is why I applied for this job.

Chairman Thank you. First of all, here you are only going to market and sell various grades of cement being manufactured by us. You have mentioned in your resume (indicating the resume lying in front of him) that you have been selling cement also, besides other construction materials. Can you tell me the difference between 43 Grade and 53 Grade cement? In what kind of construction is each of these grades of cement used?

Kulwant (confidently) Yes, Sir. These two grades of cement differ in their compression strength after setting. The 53 Grade cement has a higher strength and is used in RCC and pre-stressed concrete of higher grades, cement grouts, instant plugging mortars, etc where initial higher strength is the criteria. On the other hand, 43 Grade Cement is commonly used for plastering works, non-RCC structures, pathways etc where initial setting time is not of importance. Accordingly this grade is about 2-3% cheaper than 53 Grade cement.

Member 2 Okay. I have a problem which you can solve. Imagine that I am a distributor or dealer who is selling very little quantity of your company's cement for the last few months, although I had been selling much larger quantities earlier. How will you convince me to sell your company's cement in larger quantities?

Kulwant Madam, now that you are my customer, I will address you accordingly. I am making some assumptions about the company's marketing policies while talking to you as a customer.

(Kulwant changes his tone and speaks as if he is addressing a customer) Madam, you have been one of our most valuable dealers of various grades of cement last year, but during the first few months of this year, your orders have reduced drastically, even though the construction season is at its peak. Last year you used to lift an average of 6 tons per month, but now I see that it has reduced to less than 2 tons per month.You must be aware of our current marketing policy, in which we offer a quantity discount to our dealers provided they lift an average of 5 tons per month over a period of one year. Why don't you take advantage of this? Besides, we offer free consultancy on how to use our various grades of cement productively. Lastly, we are prepared to consider offering credit to dealers who guarantee lifting a minimum quantity of various grades of cement on a monthly basis. The last condition is negotiable based on mutually agreed terms.I am sure that considering all these incentives, you will once again start selling as much quantity of our cement as last year or even more. (concludes)

Member 2 Thank you, Kulwant. I notice that you are fluent in English. However, many of our distributors and dealers here cannot speak or understand English very well. How's your Hindi communication?

Kulwant Madam, I's a local person and so can speak Hindi as well as Haryanvi fluently. When I visit my parents, I speak to them mostly in Haryanvi. When I visit a customer, I speak in the language he is comfortable with. This establishes a good rapport with him and enables us to understand better the issues he has with our company.

Member 1 Mr Sareen, you mentioned in your sales presentation to our interview board member about offering credit. What other incentives should the company offer to dealers to sell more of their products?

Kulwant Sir, there are a number of incentive schemes and systems in the market. The most common one is the quantity discount offered to dealers and distributors. Another incentive scheme offered by some companies is a contest in which a brand new car or some such big prize is offered to the winner who sells the maximum. Some companies offer a trip to Dubai or Singapore to dealers who sell more than a certain quantity of their costlier products like 53 Grade cement. There are many similar attractive incentives to dealers for selling more.

Chairman Okay, we understand. The job vacancy we advertised requires extensive travelling in the city and suburbs to book orders. How do you plan to arrange this?

Kulwant Sir, I own a Honda Motorcycle which I am using in my current job. This will enable me to move quickly and efficiently from one dealer to the next. I assume that the company will reimburse my fuel and maintenance expenses on my business travelling.

Chairman Yes, the company has a travel expenses reimbursement system for the marketing staff. So you needn't worry about that. One last question: you have not informed us of your expectations regarding salary. What salary do you expect and how soon can you join?

Kulwant Sir, in my resume I have mentioned my current salary. This is a consolidated amount and there are no other benefits except reimbursement of my travel expenses. I will join your organisation if I am offered at least 10% to 15% more than this. Regarding my joining time, I can be relieved from my present employer within 15 days, as there is nothing about the notice period given to me in writing. But I don?t want to spoil relations with him, as I may have to deal with him in future. I know that he is one the best distributors of your cement.

Chairman Thank you, Mr Sareen. In case you are selected, we will inform you. Good day.

Kulwant (gets up from the chair and shakes hands with all the committee members). Thank you, Sir. Thank you, Madam. Good day.

(He turns around and leaves the room with a confident air and shuts the door behind him.)

7. SAMPLE INTERVIEW FOR SALES EXECUTIVE

The job of Sales Executive is an officer level post in the Sales / Marketing Department of various manufacturers, service industries, retailers and Industrial organisations. They are the key point of contact between an organisation and its customers.

Mr Zafar Iqbal is a 26 year old MBA in Marketing from University of Hyderabad with a BA from Osmania University. After passing his MBA, he worked as a Management Trainee in the Marketing Department of a Kanpur based medium sized company manufacturing and selling personal care products like hair oil, talcum powder, skin creams etc. After completing his one year training period, Zafar was absorbed as a Sales Officer in the same company. He has now been working on this post or more than one year.

He is smartly dressed in a well pressed suit and tie along with well-polished formal black shoes.

As soon as his name is announced, he confidently moves to the closed door of the interview room. He knocks on the door and then opens it. Three persons are sitting at the far end of a large office table in the centre of the room, out of which the person on the left side is a woman.

Zafar (addressing the man in the centre) May I come in, Sir? Yes, Mr Iqbal, you may come in. (pointing to the candidate's chair) Take your seat.

Zafar (sitting down) Thank you, Sir. Good morning to all of you.

Member 1 Good morning, Zafar. Your CV does not reveal much about the nature of your work experience. Can you elaborate on that?

Zafar (making eye contact one by one with all three interviewers) Madam, I did not realise that you would require more details, as I actually have just over one year's actual work experience in selling personal care products. The first four months of the one year I was a Management Trainee in the company consisted of a long Induction Programme. During this time, they rotated me, along with six other Management Trainees, in all the departments of the company to enable us to understand how the company works. The last department in which we were sent was Sales. For the next eight months, I spent two months each in the Sales Department of each of the four divisions of the company, just learning the ropes. At the end, I was placed as a Sales Officer in their Talcum Powder Division and have been selling talcum powder since then.For the last 15 months I have been covering the district of Aligarh in UP where we have 2 distributors, 30 dealers and about 120 stockists for selling various types of our brand of talcum powder. I interact with the distributors almost every day either through visits or through the phone to pick up orders or solve any product distribution problems faced by them. I visit each dealer at least twice every month and every stockist every month, particularly to boost sales of products which are moving sluggishly. I also convey to them all necessary information given by our Head Office at Kanpur. As our terms with the distributors are advance payment against orders, I don't have to deal with payment issues.(concluding) In summary, this is my current work profile.

Chairman Thank you, Zafar. I notice that your home is in Hyderabad. Yet, you have decided to work so far from home. Don't you ever feel homesick?

Zafar Sir, I agree that I have spent most of my life in Hyderabad. However, when I was selected by my present employer based on a campus interview, I felt that it would be a golden chance to build an outstanding career. I feel that the attraction of home should not interfere with our work. We should be willing to work anywhere, provided the work is interesting and the compensation attractive. I rarely feel homesick, but when I do, I phone my mother and tell her what I learnt that day.

Member 2 It means that you are willing to work anywhere. You may be aware that we are operating throughout India. Suppose we post you to a district in Bengal, will you join us? Also, what preparations should you make for working there?

Zafar Yes, Sir, I will definitely join your company. It will give me another opportunity to hone my selling skills. My major preparation for working in Bengal will be to learn the Bengali language, both spoken as well as written. This will be vital for effective communication with the dealers and distributors there. I am comfortable with Bengali food, as many items are common to Hyderabadi food with minor variations.

Chairman (interrupts) I think we are digressing from the main topics to be covered in the interview. Zafar, during your 15 months career of selling talcum powder in Aligarh district, can you highlight a major problem that you sorted out to the satisfaction of all concerned?

Zafar Yes, Sir. Although problems keep on occurring and we keep on solving them, I personally contributed in a major way to solve a serious problem that resulted in many complaints from our dealers and customers which occurred last year. The problem was less weight of powder in the 400 gram packing of our Jasmine perfumed talcum powder. Some of the packets had only between 300 and 375 grams of powder! Initially we did not believe these complaints, but when they were reported from many dealers in my district, I visited all such dealers and even customer's homes to collect such defective packets. In going through the labels on the packets, I found that all of them had the same batch no and date of manufacture. Immediately, I informed the Head Office about the results of my investigation. On inspecting the records at our factory, which are meticulously maintained as we are ISO 9000 compliant, it was found that the powder dispensing mechanism had become inoperative for about 15 minutes on the date of manufacture printed on the packing and had been dispensing less than the required quantity. Subsequently the fault was rectified, but about 120 defective packets were packed during this time. That full batch had been delivered to one of our Aligarh distributors, who had supplied individual packs to dealers and stockists. Finally our management sent a gift pack of talcum powder along with an apology letter to all affected customers and dealers as a free replacement.

Member 1 Congratulations, Zafar. You kept your customers satisfied. Now tell me, how do you travel all over the district? Do you have your own vehicle?

Zafar Madam, after I became a Sales Officer, the company offered me a new motorcycle on a loan to be paid back over one year in monthly instalments. Now that the loan has been paid in full, the motorcycle is owned by me.

Chairman One last question, Mr Iqbal. We have not discussed about your compensation and joining time. What are you expecting and when can you join?

Zafar Sir, in my resume I have mentioned my current salary as well as the formula of incentive for increased sales applicable to me. The incentive, which is the variable component of my salary payable annually, has worked out at almost 40% of the fixed component of my salary this year due to my good performance. I hope your company has a similar package for staff in Sales. Regarding my joining time, I need to give one month's notice to my present employer according to the terms of the appointment letter. I would like to leave them without any hard feelings from either side. Don't worry, Mr Iqbal. We'll take good care of you. In case you are selected, we will inform you suitably. Good day.(gets up from the chair and shakes hands with the committee members). Thank you, Sir. Thank you, Sir. Thank you, Madam. Good day.

(He turns around and leaves the room with a confident air and shuts the door behind him.)

8. SAMPLE INTERVIEW FOR SALES MANAGER

A Sales Manager is responsible for meeting the sales targets of the company employing him through effective planning and execution. Sales managers' responsibilities vary with the size of the organisation they work for.

Abhijit Ghosh is a 34 year old MBA in Marketing from a management institution in Bengaluru after completing his Mechanical Engineering degree from NIT, Patna. His total work experience of 9 years has been in Sales and Marketing of products related to the agricultural and automotive sectors. He has been called for an interview for the Post of Sales Manager responsible for the Eastern Region (covering East and North-East India) sales and service of a tractor manufacturing company in the private sector.

When his name is announced, he confidently moves to tthe interview room. A committee of three men and a woman are sitting at the far end of a large office table in the centre of the room. He gently knocks on the door for getting permission to enter.

Abhijit (addressing the person who appears to be the eldest and in charge) May I come in, Sir?

Chairman Yes, Mr Ghosh. (pointing to the candidate's chair) Please come in and sit down.

Abhijit (sitting down and glancing around) Thank you, Sir. Good morning to all of you.

Lady I will introduce the panel members. Mr Sushil Lamba (indicating the Chairman) is our Marketing Director. Mr Sadanand Gopinath (indicating Member 1) is our Head of Sales. Mr EC Krishnan (indicating Member 2) is our Head of Service. I am Lakshmi Vishwanath, HR Manager. Now let's start the interview. Mr Ghosh, your resume has highlighted an important point. During your career of 9 years, you have worked in three companies, all in different fields of operation. Now you want to change once again. What is the reason for this instability?

Abhijit Madam, pardon me, but my first year of employment was only as a Management Trainee. After finishing my training in the public sector tractor manufacturing organisation in Haryana, I was released. After that I joined the Sales Department of an organised sector organisation manufacturing agricultural pumps with its headquarters in Faridabad. I worked there for five years in the Sales Department with postings in Assam (3 years) and Jharkhand (2 years). When the business of this organisation shrank due to change in management,, which occurred due to the company being purchased by a multinational, I realised it was time to move on, as they were about to wind up the pumps division due to poor response of customers. Soon I found a job as Assistant Manger (Sales and Service) of a startup company importing and selling tractors in India. Two years ago, I was promoted as Deputy Manager in this company and made head of Eastern Region Sales covering West Bengal, Bihar, Jharkhand and Odisha. However, the sales of this company are limited because they only sell high power tractors, 65 HP and above capacity, which are not much in demand by farmers due to their cost. I now feel that my career is suffering due to this problem and so want to join mainstream sales, at which your company is successful in Northern and Western India.

Chairman Okay, Mr Ghosh. We understand the predicament you are in. Since you have worked in the Eastern region and also the North-East, we are interested in hiring a person to head the tractor sales in this region where we plan to market our products starting next month. Can you tell us how you will organise this?

Abhijit (confidently) Definitely, Sir. I am familiar with the market there and understand very well that in this region most of the farmers are small or medium level farmers. That is why high power tractors, which cost very much, will not have a good market. Farmers here mostly require 25 HP and 35 HP tractors, not higher power than these. My plan for this market is to have one main dealer in each state located at the capital of the state. This dealer will have a few sub-dealers located in various major cities and towns in the state. For a large state like West Bengal, there may be eight to ten sub-dealers, whereas for a smaller state there may be four or five sub-dealers.

In the smaller states in the North-East, there may be just one sub-dealer in each state controlled by the main dealer either in Guwahati or Shillong.The main dealer and sub-dealers may be appointed based on their past record of sales of capital goods products to the farmers and their reputation in the area concerned. We should not appoint dealers who are not professionals in this line, as it may affect initial sales. All the dealers must be financially sound with a good past record of prompt payment for supplies. An important aspect in tractor sales is the service provided to the customer. Each sub-dealer will have a full-time resident tractor technician or engineer who has been trained in our factory on all operation and maintenance procedures for each of the models. The main dealer in each state will appoint a Service Incharge who will also coordinate supply of spares and consumables to the sub-dealers and customers.

Member 1 (interrupting) Fine. We understand how you are planning the sales and service network. But, tell me, how will you set the sales targets for each state and each sub-dealer? Is target setting not important for increasing sales?

Abhijit (turning towards Member 1) Yes, Sir. I was coming to that. For increasing sales, we must have an incentive programme for the dealers. Besides their normal commission on each tractor sold, both the main dealer and the sub-dealers should be given an additional amount, whether in cash or kind, for sales over and above the target set for them. These targets should be set in discussion with the dealers themselves every quarter. Our marketing team can visit each state in turn and hold a dealer's meet at the main dealer's location to set the targets. Based on our annual plan of sales for the Eastern region, we should decide the rough target for each state and inform our expectation in the dealer meet. This can be then discussed and the target for each sub-dealer should be finalised.

Member 2 You have told us about dealer appointments and targets. What marketing staff members are you planning to have and on what basis will you select the incumbents?

Abhijit (turning towards Member 2) Yes, Sir, I had thought of the staff I will require. In each state I will have a Sales Officer or Sales Engineer who will also be responsible, besides the main dealer, for achieving the quarterly sales targets for that state. He will also earn an incentive for sales more than the target. Each Sales Officer may have one or two Sales Representatives working under him to cover the state completely. The Sales Officer will also have a Service and Spares Coordinator with him to look after the Service aspect of the business. This coordinator will be a technical person who will attend to any service related problems of customers which have not been solved at the dealer level. I will also tour each state at least once every month to ensure proper coordination between our staff, the main dealers and sub-dealers. I will also have one Coordinator in my office at Eastern Region Headquarters to ensure that shipments from the factory reach the main dealers and sub-dealers in time. This Coordinator will also ensure timely supply of spare parts and consumables from the factory to the region,

Chairman Mr Ghosh, have you thought about the payment terms for the main dealer and the sub-dealers for supply of the tractors as well as the spare parts and consumables?

Abhijit Sir, as the company is already selling tractors in two regions of India, whatever payment policy it is following in these regions should also be followed here, otherwise it may create a problem. However, the normal policy in this industry is that the main dealer pays the full price of the tractors while placing the order for supply. The main dealer may have different payment terms with different sub-dealers; we will not interfere with that. It depends on many factors which are not in our control. However, we can mediate between the main dealer and any sub-dealer if there is a payment dispute between them.

Lady (looking around at all the Board members) I think you have covered all aspects of the marketing of our tractors in the Eastern Region. However, we have not yet discussed your compensation. What are your expectations?

Abhijit Madam, I have indicated in my resume my current compensation. The variable component, i.e. the incentive and bonus, have been separately mentioned. Regarding the fixed component of my salary, I will join your organisation if I am offered at least 10% to 15% more than my current fixed component of salary. The variable component may be decided, in discussion with you, based on the target given to me.

Chairman I get the idea. We will discuss it once we decide to appoint you, as an appointment at this level requires the concurrence of our Managing Director. He may want to meet you next week. One more point; how soon can you join? We plan to launch sales in the Eastern Region next month.

Abhijit Chairman Abhijit Sir, in my resume I have mentioned that the notice period in my present employment is 30 days. If I want to leave earlier, it will not be ethical and also will spoil relations with them. They may also deduct my salary proportionately. But you can be sure that from the moment I join, I will take all the required steps to have an early launch of sales so that we don't miss the main sales season.

Chairman Thank you, Mr Ghosh. We will inform you when our MD may want to meet you. Good day.

Abhijit (gets up from the chair and shakes hands with all the committee members). Thank you, Sir. Thank you, Madam. Good day.

(He turns around and leaves the room with a confident air and shuts the door behind him.)

9. SAMPLE INTERVIEW FOR IT COORDINATOR

An IT Coordinator is responsible for determining, developing and implementing an organisation's information technology requirements. His activities can include reviewing and solving internal help requests and monitoring computer performance for potential problems. IT coordinators may also provide an organisation with day-to-day computer support, such as installing basic software and providing updates.

Kamal Gopalakrishnan is a 28 year old B Tech in Computer Science from a National Institute of Technology (NIT). He worked for 2 years as a Service Engineer in a computer networking organisation, where he also acquired the CCNA qualification. For the last 3 years he has been working as the Head of IT in a medium sized manufacturing company which has computerised most of its paperwork related to Purchasing, Accounting, HR, Administration, Sales and Service. When his name is announced, Kamal confidently moves to the open door. He gently knocks on the door for getting permission to enter.

Kamal (looking at the man sitting in the centre) May I come in, Sir?

Chairman Yes, Mr Gopalakrishnan, you may come in. (pointing to the candidate's chair) Please take your seat.

Kamal (sitting down) Thank you, Sir. Good morning to all of you.

Member 1 Mr Gopalakrishnan, tell me what you have been doing after you completed your engineering degree.

Kamal (looking around and making eye contact one by one with all three interviewers) Yes, Sir. While I was in the final year of my degree, I looked for a job which would utilise my technical skills. I was selected as a Service Engineer which was installing computer networks and maintaining them. Side by side, I acquired the CCNA qualification through a part-time course, as this qualification is essential in this line. After working in this company for two years, I was approached through some contacts by a manufacturing organisation which was just starting to computerise its entire paperwork. They wanted me to set up their computer systems and networking with a suitable ERP (Enterprise Resource Planning) system.

As the offer was attractive and giving me an opportunity for a wider field of operation, I shifted to this company. During the next one year, I set up their entire ERP System from scratch with the assistance of two engineers working under my guidance. During this time, I often worked long hours in installing and servicing the hardware and troubleshooting the software to ensure that the systems were up and running. Soon I was rewarded with being designated as Head of IT Since then, I have been continuing the routine maintenance and service of the entire computer network in the company to the satisfaction of the company management as well as the users. (pauses)

Member 2 Then why do you want to change your job, Mr Gopalakrishnan, when you are satisfied with it? Are you not happy there?

Kamal Sir, I am always looking for challenges, whether technical or managerial. Your company is a bigger one than my current employer and I am sure I will be able to make a significant contribution to your diversification operations and also enhance my knowledge and experience suitably.(As he pauses, the Chairman of the interview board interrupts.)

Chairman So you know about our diversification plans. (he looks around at the other two members) It appears it is no longer a secret. (addressing the candidate) Actually, Kamal, we are looking for a person to head our computerisation in the new division we are setting up. If you can carry this out without serious problems over the next few months, we may ask you to head the IT operations of the entire company. So tell us what major considerations you would take into account while computerising the new division, which includes its own manufacturing plant and separate sales and service operations.

Kamal Yes, Sir. There are three basic considerations. This is based on my observation that your current operations are not networked; the computerisation is through stand-alone systems carrying out routine duties like creating, printing, copying etc. I believe that even your accounting software is standalone. These three considerations are regarding hardware, software i.e. which ERP to select, and lastly networking. First I will explain about the hardware. The normal configuration used with ERP systems is the thin client configuration. This means that there is a major server on which the ERP is installed and all the computers terminals are just dumb terminals with no storage or computation facilities. This is the best configuration for using ERP effectively. Next I will explain about the software, i.e. the ERP system. Generally such licensed systems are costly and users need to be trained for using them effectively for generating reports, answering queries and many other necessary tasks. The selection of the

ERP will be based on the size of the new division we are computerising, but it must also be able to expand to the size necessary later on for the organisation as a whole. Lastly, I will tell you about the networking. This is the simplest of all. Hard wire networks will be installed at each location like the plant, the Head Office and the various sales offices. Servers at each of these locations will be linked to the main server at the Head Office through wireless networking. This configuration is the most cost effective and most reliable, considering the number of Sales Offices all over the country. I have implemented such a system on a smaller scale with my current employer and it is running successfully.

Member 1 Thank you. Can you cite any particular problem which you solved in your current organisation using your technical knowledge and problem-solving skills?

Kamal Yes, Sir, there are many such cases, but I will mention a recent problem which perplexed us initially, but was solved after careful consideration of the technical matters involved. Recently we had upgraded our version of ERP. One computer system, which had been disconnected when an employee left the company before the upgradation, did not have its corresponding software upgraded in the server because the server did not detect its presence.

When a new employee joined after the upgradation, this system was again connected. However, it did not work properly despite all efforts by my engineers. I was asked to look into the problem. When I checked the software code for this system in the server, I realised that the code had not been upgraded. On upgrading the code to the new version, the system started working properly.

Member 2 Mr Gopalakrishnan, you have not given us an idea about what salary you expect. What are your expectations and how soon can you join?

Kamal Sir, in my resume I have mentioned my current salary and CTC (Cost-to-Company). I expect at least 10% better than this, as the work area will be larger. My notice period in my present organisation is one month, but I may be able to get it reduced to 20 days by adjusting my leave entitlement against the notice period. I am not engaged in any critical activity there at the moment, so I do not visualise any problem from my employer's side on this matter.

Chairman Thank you, Kamal. In case you are selected, we will inform you suitably. Good day.

Kamal (gets up from the chair and shakes hands with all the committee members). Thank you, Sir. Good day.

(He turns around, goes though the door and shuts it behind him.)

10. SAMPLE INTERVIEW FOR SCHOOL TEACHER

A school teacher performs a variety of daily duties include leading classes, working with individual students, planning lessons and marking assignments. Teachers are also responsible for forming and enforcing classroom rules.

Namita Bisht is a 25 year old graduate in Arts (History, Geography and Political Science) from a State University. She has passed her B Ed exam with first division two years ago. Since then, she has been teaching Social Studies to Class VI, VII and VIII students in an elementary school in a small town. Recently she has appeared for the CTET exam, but the results had not yet been declared when she appeared for this interview.

When her name is announced, she moves to the open door of the interview room. Three people are sitting at the far end of a large office table in the centre of the room. The man in the centre appears to be in charge of the interview. The other members of the committee are women who are sitting on either side of the man. Namita gently knocks on the door for getting permission to enter.

Namita May I come in, Sir? Yes, Ms Bisht. (pointing to the candidate's chair) Sit down.

Namita (sitting down) Thank you, Sir. Good morning to all of you.

Member 1 Namita, tell me what subject you teach best?

Namita (looking around and making eye contact one by one with all three interviewers) Madam, I'm currently teaching all Social Science subjects to Class VI to VIII students in the elementary school where I am working. I like all these subjects equally. History has many interesting stories which I teach my students by telling them the events in story book form. Geography tells us very interesting facts about our Earth and other natural phenomena. I often explain these phenomena to the students by taking them outside the classroom and showing them these phenomena practically. Regarding Political Science, I sometimes bring newspapers to the class to illustrate examples of the concepts I teach because the newspapers are full of political news every day. Economics is the only subject in Class IX and X which I do not teach because it is not part of the Elementary School syllabus. (pauses)

Chairman You have an interesting method of teaching! Anyway, now tell me why you applied for this job.

Namita Sir, I know that the post advertised is for a TGT, which is better paid than what I get in my current job. It will give me an opportunity to advance my career, as your school is CBSE affiliated. In addition, if I succeed in clearing the CTET exam which I have recently attempted, my career prospects will be even better than before. I feel I have done very well in the CTET exam and expect to clear it. I had prepared the Child Psychology very diligently and I'm confident I will score high in that section.

Member 2 Interesting! Now that you are talking about child psychology, you can answer a question from your teaching experience. Tell me, did you ever face a persistent disciplinary problem in any of your classes? If so, how did you tackle it?

Namita (thinks for a few seconds and then speaks) Yes, Ma'am. This occurred last year in one section of Class VIII in my school. A 14 year old boy used to repeatedly play pranks on the other students when I was writing something on the board, as I could not spot him doing so when my back was turned. After receiving repeated complaints from other students about him, I set a trap for him. I pretended to punish a student (after briefing her about what to do) by asking her to stand near the blackboard but facing the other students. I had asked the girl to indicate to me with a wave of her hand when the boy was about to play the prank. While writing on the board, when her signal came, I immediately turned around and caught the boy red-handed. I did not punish him in front of other students, but after the class was over and during the break, I called the boy to the Teachers' Common Room and counselled him. It turned out that he did not understand anything of what I was teaching because he had missed some important classes for a few days when his mother fell ill and there was nobody at home to look after her. That is why he was passing his time playing pranks. That same evening after school, I visited the boy's home and talked to his mother. I suggested to her to allow the boy to stay back for one hour after school for a few days so that I could tutor him on the missed topics. Thus, the pranks were stopped and the boy was grateful to me for solving his problem.

Member 2 Thank you, Namita. You feel you can continue in a similarly active manner in our school also?

Namita Certainly Ma'am, why not? If my students have their problems solved, they will do better in their exams. Here I will have to work harder because I have to prepare students for the Board exams. But I'm willing to take it up as a challenge.

Chairman One thing, Ms Bisht. I notice that you are fluent in English. How did you develop this fluency?

Namita Sir, it is all there in my resume. You will notice that I have studied throughout in the English medium. My schooling was completed in a missionary school where the teachers were very strict about grammatically correct written and spoken English. They made us speak to the teachers only in English (except in the Hindi classes). Gradually I developed fluency in English. Of course, while teaching, I switch to Hindi to better explain some concept to the students. This comes naturally to me.

Chairman You should understand regarding the salary which will be paid here. Initially we will give you a consolidated amount which is much better than what you are presently getting. After six months and, subject to your clearing the CTET exam, we will offer you the TGT scale given to other teachers. If that is fine with you, tell me when you can join our school as a Social Science teacher.

Namita Sir, the summer holidays are starting next week. I can join your school on 1st of July or whenever the school opens after the summer holidays.

Chairman That is fine. We will send the appointment letter to your residential address when the Board of Governors of the school approves your appointment. Good day.Good day to you, Sir.(turning towards each of the ladies) Good day, Madam. Thank you.

(She turns around and leaves the room with a confident air and shuts the door behind her.)

ADMISSION INTERVIEWS

- *Interview for BHM Course*
- *Interview for MBA Course*
- *Interview for Masters in Journalism*

Here we are providing some mock interviews for the admission courses. These sample interviews will provide an insight into types of questions asked in such interviews. Questions asked may be course specific and general also.

1. SAMPLE INTERVIEW FOR BHM COURSE

A degree of Bachelor in Hotel Management (BHM) is usually given on completing 4 years of study after passing class XII. This industry includes the categories of Travel & Tourism (e.g. airlines), Accommodation (e.g. hotels) and Food & Beverage (e.g. restaurants).

The test may include some general knowledge questions on the hospitality industry. Some colleges also hold a Group Discussion (GD) before selecting candidates for the Personal Interview (PI). In both GD and PI, fluency in the language of instruction and good communication skills are tested.

Shambhu Chatterjee is an 18 year old Class XII passed student in Science (Physics, Chemistry and Biology) from a CBSE school. He is well-dressed in a light shirt, dark trousers and a tie to go with them. He is clean shaven and has a confident smile on his face.

When his name is announced, he moves to the open door of the interview room. Three gentlemen are sitting at a large office table in the centre of the room. The man in the centre appears to be in charge of the interview. The other members of the committee are sitting on either side of him. There is a white board on the right side of the room. Shambhu gently knocks on the door for getting permission to enter.

Shambhu May I come in, Sir? Yes, Mr Chatterjee. (pointing to the candidate's chair) Sit down.

Shambhu (sitting down) Thank you, Sir. Good morning to all of you.

Member 1 Shambhu, tell me what subject you liked best in Class XII. Also tell me the reason.

Shambhu (looking around and making eye contact one by one with all three interviewers) Sir, I liked Chemistry best. I was always fascinated with the chemical composition of various compounds, especially organic compounds which have specific structures. I loved conducting various experiments in the Chemistry Lab. It was my favourite laboratory.

Chairman Interesting. Can you give the name and chemical composition of a well-known cyclic compound? Also draw its structure on the board here. (hands over a marker pen to him and points to the white board on the right side)

Shambhu Yes, Sir. The cyclic compound is benzene and its formula is C_6H_6. (gets up and draws it on the board). This is its structure, Sir.

Member 2 Good. If you are so much interested in Chemistry, why don't you go for BSc? Why try for Hotel Management?

Shambhu (thinks for a few seconds and then speaks) I will tell you the reason, Sir. Doing B Sc and M Sc may be able to get me work either as a research associate in a University or a job in an industry related to chemicals or pharmaceuticals. But both these jobs are not as well paid in India as a job in the hospitality industry, especially with a qualification from a highly reputed institution like yours. Further, as I want to ultimately become a chef by specialising in Food and Beverages, I will use my knowledge and interest in Chemistry to prepare more hygienic and nutritious meals for my guests. I will be able to get highly paid jobs in 5-star hotels and other premium hospitality establishments with a degree from your instituition.

Member 2 You have mentioned the term 'hospitality' just now. What do you understand by hospitality in terms of hotel industry?

Shambhu Certainly, Sir. Hospitality actually means, 'taking care of guests in the best possible way'. In terms of hotel industry it means organising and providing services and taking care of guests in a friendly and generous manner. Hospitality industry includes all establishments involved in providing services for guests. They provide more mental satisfaction than just tangible objects.

Member 1 Shambhu, you have expressed your interest in becoming a chef, i.e. you want to specialise in catering. What do you understand by catering?

Shambhu Sir, catering refers to food and drinks, whereas catering industry refers to hospitality industry that provides food and beverage items. A catering establishment is an organisation which provides food with an objective to satisfy its customer. There are two aspects to catering: one is provision of the desired food and beverages and the other is proper service.

Chairman One last question, Mr Chatterjee. Why do you want to join our institution for pursuing the BHM course?

Shambhu Sir, it is well-known that your institution has been producing the finest graduates in this profession who have risen to be Head Chef or Chief Manager of various famous international hotel chains. I also want to be one like them.

Chairman OK. We will inform you if and when you are selected. Good day.

Shambhu Good day to you, Sir. (turning towards each of the other members). Thank you.

(He turns around and leaves the room with a confident air and shuts the door behind him.)

2. SAMPLE INTERVIEW FOR MBA COURSE

The minimum qualification required for entry to an MBA course is graduation in any discipline and a satisfactory score in a standardised aptitude test like CAT, MAT, XAT etc. The colleges offering MBA also hold a Group Discussion (GD) before selecting candidates the Personal Interview (PI). In both GD and PI, fluency in the language of instruction and good communication skills are tested.

Ravi Saluja is a 22 year old BBA (Bachelor of Business Administration) graduate from a State University. After graduation, Ravi has been working as an Excise Clerk in a factory producing assembled consumer items for about one year. He attempted the CAT and scored 90 percentile in it.

He is well dressed in a formal suit with tie and appears cheerful and optimistic. When his name is announced, he moves to the open door of the interview room. Two people are sitting at the far end of a large office table in the centre of the room. The man on the left is older and appears to be in charge of the interview. Ravi gently knocks on the door for getting permission to enter.

Ravi May I come in, Sir?

Member Yes, you may come in Mr Saluja. (pointing to the candidate's chair) Sit down.

Ravi (sitting down) Thank you, Sir. Good morning to both of you.

Member Ravi, I observe from your bio-data that you are working as an excise clerk in a factory. Why do you want to leave a job to join the MBA programme?

Ravi (making eye contact one by one with both interviewers) Sir, I agree that I will leave the job if I get admission to your college's MBA programme. After finishing my BBA, I took up a job, as my father had retired from service. I also wanted to prepare for the CAT exam, as my ultimate aim was to complete MBA, so that I can build up a career and achieve something in life. As the job was a routine one, I had enough time to prepare for the CAT exam. I can say that I succeeded in my efforts, as I have cleared the CAT as well as the GD conducted by you. (pauses)

Chairman I notice that you scored 90 percentile in CAT. Do you consider this a good score?

Ravi Certainly, Sir. It means that I have done better that 90% of the other candidates who gave the CAT this time. I also understand that you also consider it a good score, otherwise you would not have called me for the GD.

Member Good! Now tell me about your job? What work do you do there?

Ravi Yes, Sir. My first duty is to ensure that all the components of Excise Duty paid by the company on raw materials and bought out components used in assembling the finished products are entered in the accounting software used by us. The second part of the job is to enter in the accounting software the Excise Duty paid on the finished products being despatched for sale. Once this is paid, we can claim reimbursement of the Excise Duty paid on raw materials and bought out components. My final job is to deal with Excise Inspectors when they visit us for an audit.

Chairman You seem to know your job. But with the implementation of Goods and Services Tax (GST), will this change?

Ravi Certainly, Sir. In fact, we are in the process of installing the new software on our systems. Implementation of GST will be beneficial to our industry, as earlier we could not claim refund of the Sales Tax paid on raw materials and bought out components via the Sales Tax paid by us on our finished products. But with GST, we can claim all such charges paid.

Chairman You seem to be well aware of the implications of GST, Mr Saluja. But how will you support your studies, as your father cannot contribute much?

Ravi Sir, I discussed this matter with my father before attending this interview. He has taken up a job in the private sector which will help. Besides, once I get your admission letter, I will approach a nationalised bank for an educational loan. I am confident that my loan will be sanctioned due to my academic record and the reputation of your college. I know that your campus placements are envied by many other colleges which award MBA degrees.

Member You seem to be very confident of being selected. Any reason?

Ravi Not really, Sir. I can only say that my father will be happy if I am selected for the course. He has always motivated me to acquire a qualification which will help me to build a career.

Chairman I understand. We will inform you very soon about your selection. Good day.

Ravi Good day to you, Sir. (turning towards the interview board member) Good day, Sir. Thank you.

(He turns around and leaves the room with a confident air and shuts the door behind him.)

3. SAMPLE INTERVIEW FOR MASTERS IN JOURNALISM

A post graduate degree in MA (Mass Communication) or MA (Journalism) is given by a University on completing 2 years of study after graduation.

The minimum qualification required for entry to such courses is graduation in any discipline and a satisfactory score in a standardised test to test candidates' aptitude and written communication skills. The colleges offering such courses also hold a Group Discussion (GD) before selecting candidates for the Personal Interview (PI). In both GD and PI, fluency in the language of instruction and good communication skills are tested.

Ms Shailaja Verma is a 21 year old graduate in Economics from a Central University. She is well dressed in formal Western wear with a white shirt, black trousers and a silk scarf around the neck. She is well poised with a confident smile on her face.

When her name is announced, she moves to the open door of the interview room. Two gentlemen and a lady are sitting at a large office table in the room. The man in the centre appears to be in charge of the interview. The other members of the committee are sitting on either side of him. Shailaja gently knocks on the door for getting permission to enter.

Shailaja May I come in, Sir?

Chairman Yes, Ms Verma. (pointing to the candidate's chair) Take your seat.

Shailaja (sitting down) Thank you, Sir. Good morning to all of you.

Lady Member Shailaja, I observe from your CV that you have graduated in Economics with very good marks. Then why did you apply for this journalism course?

Shailaja (looking around and making eye contact one by one with all three interviewers) Madam, I love interacting with people and understanding their views. I am also very interested in Economics. I felt that I can pursue both interests if I take up a career in financial journalism. The scope of this branch of journalism has gone up manifold since the time that TV news channels started and with the growth of the internet. To ensure that my career gives me satisfaction in future, I felt that a professional qualification is essential. That is why I applied for this course.

Chairman Fine. Now let us know your views about the media. What is the role of newspapers in society, now that the electronic media has overshadowed them?

Shailaja Yes, Sir. Newspapers play multiple roles in society. First, they keep the people aware of the activities of the government. Further, newspapers shape and influence the views, opinions and attitudes of millions of readers throughout the nation and the world. They also mobilise public opinion and play an important role in fighting the menace of corruption. They are the guardians of liberty, civic and human rights in the world. Besides this, they promote commerce, trade and business through the advertisements published by them. The radio and TV channels may have many other attractions, but the inquisitive nature of man remains unfulfilled till he goes through the columns of newspapers every morning.

Member 2 Yes, Yes, that's enough. Now tell us what you expect from this course.

Shailaja (thinks for a few seconds and then speaks) Yes, Sir. First, I expect to sharpen my journalistic skills. As you must have seen in my CV, I was the editor of the students' monthly magazine 'The Spark' in my college for two years. At that time I realised that I had a lot to learn in this line. I used to write the Editorial and at least one article in each issue, but without any professional guidance. Thus I was unhappy about the results. Although the magazine was popular because it raised many student issues, I felt that it could have been much better. That is what motivated me to join this course. I observe from your curriculum that you have courses on Digital Media, Financial Journalism and Online Journalism. All these are of interest to me. Your brochure also mentions that have three famous TV and print journalists as your guest speakers. I will be very happy when they pass on their tips for success to us. So I expect a lot from this course.

Lady Member One last question, Shailaja. What are the qualities which a good journalist should possess to be successful?

Shailaja Madam, there are many such qualities, but creativity is the most prized quality in this line. It enables you to find opportunities which do not exist for others. Besides this, hard work, willingness and capacity to learn, teamwork and effective communication skills are important for growth in this field. Belief in oneself, coupled with the ability of not taking oneself too seriously, will definitely take one places. And ....

Chairman (interrupting) I think that is enough. We will inform you if and when you are selected. Good day.

Shailaja Good day to you, Sir. (turning towards each of the other members) Good day, Madam. Good day, Sir. Thank you.

(She turns around and leaves the room with a confident air and shuts the door behind her.)

SOME MYTHS ABOUT INTERVIEW

Each member make his/her own comments and submit the result of candidate to concerned authority.

MYTH 1 **An Interview is about how a candidate can prove him/her self.**

An Interview provides an opportunity to the candidate to meet and talk to the prospective employer and ask questions to get information. It is not just proving one self.

MYTH 2 **The more qualified person will get the job.**

The selection of a candidate depends on his performance at the time of interview. There is no guarantee that the most qualified person will get the job after an interview.

MYTH 3 **In Interview a candidate will succed if he/she is able to give perfect answers.**

It is not true. In reality in an interview, there is no perfect answer. A candidata who is able to comprehend the question well and is able to answer it smartly, is more likely to be successful.

MYTH 4 **Job candidates need to speak a lot in order to be successful in an interview.**

This is not true at all as short answers capture the interest of the interviewer. Long answer can be monotonous and boring. A candidate must be aware of what to say, how to say and when to stop talking.

MYTH 5 **All interviewers are well adept in their knowledge and they know what they are doing.**

It is not true. Sometimes interview may be taken by a person not related to field and not ask relevant questions. Candidate must try to answer the questions asked by them in such a way that they get the required information.

MYTH 6 **The condidata should never say that he/she does not know the answer.**

This is not true. In an interview nothing is worse than pretension. If the candidate does not know the answer, there is nothing wrong is admitting it. Giving a wrong answer is the worst situation.

MYTH 7 **Many people believe that one can impress the interviewers with their appearances and smart looks.**

This is totally incorrect. It is important to dress decently and to be smart but a candidate's knowledge, skill, experience and altitude matter more than appearance. Good looks alone can not make a candidate winner in the interview.

MYTH 8 **Most people think that interview always try to find flaws in a candidate.**

This is not correct. Interviewers just try to check whether a candidate is a right fit in the organisation in terms of skill, knowledge and altitude, they do not attempt to uncover a candidate's flaws or short comings.

APPLYING FOR JOB AND SAMPLE RESUMES

- *How to Apply for a Job*
- *Sample Resumes*

It is very important to apply for a job effectively. It is our resume which can make our job application more impressive if constructed in a proper and systematic way. Here are some important tips to make your job application more impressive

How to Apply for a Job?

Candidates aspiring for such jobs have to respond to these advertisement along with the brief Resumes. It is also observed that some reputed companies are advertising walk-in-interviews because these companies are no longer interested in scanning through long resumes to shortlist candidates. For the purpose of securing jobs in private sector organisations, among the most important communications you have to send the following written or scanned document to the leading organisation i.e.

- Resume
- The coverletter to accompany you resume.
- Scanned photograph and other document; according to the requirement of organisation.

RESUME WRITING

Resume is also known as Curriculam Vitae (CV) or Biodata. It explains complete background of a candidate, his education, experience, achievement and merits. In short, it is a marketing tool that outlines a candidate's skills and experience relevant to the job.

An average employer only spends a few seconds looking at a resume so it should be essentially impressive to get employer impressed with your qualification and key skills. Presently, job market is highly competitive so it is important to have a professional resume containing the right-information so that it will stand out amongst the countless other resumes. Before writing resume one must keep in mind which type of resume will be suited for him/her as not all resumes are befitting the requirements of all professions.

Types of Resume

The resumes are of four types

1. **Chronological Resume** It is a resume that list down one's work history in reverse chronological order. This type of format preferred for undergratuate. It shows the progress that a person has done either in a short time period or working in a few companies.
2. **Function Resume** It is basically used by a person who has too much or too less experienced. It focuses on skills, strengths which are important to employers but there is no detailed work history.
3. **Combination Resume** It is a good combination of the both, chronological resume and functional resume. It shows off strong employment record with special attention towards your qualities and qualification on a professional level.

How to Write a Resume?

A resume is a document that tells prospective employers exactly what you want them to know about you and why you would be a good fit for their open position. It also tells the employer that you have right experience and skills for the job.

A resume is generally written in the following format

- **Contact Information** It should be highlighted so that a hiring manager can easily get in touch with you if needed. Contact details include name, e-mail address, contact number and the home address that is optional.
- **Career Objective** A short, targeted statement that clearly outline one's career direction and simultaneously positioning you as someone who fits what the organisation looking for.
- **Educational Information** This part of resume helps to display foundation level of knowledge and academic achivements. It should be in reverse chronological order *i.e.* begin with the last qualification.
- **Employment History** While providing employment history, one should start with recent job and go backward from there. Give the job position and time period you worked there. For each job one should list the things he achieved, contribution he/she made for organisation.
- **Any Additional Skills and Information** It highlights any technical or specialised skills you have, that are applicable to the position. It should include; fluency in English as second language, knowledge of computer applications etc.

- **Extracurricular Activities and Awards** Qualities such as teamwork, leadership, discipline, responsibility etc best brought out when one participates in extracurricular activities such as sports, debates etc. Awards won in such activities are the testimony or assessment of your such qualities.
- **A Professional Summary** It is sometimes called a profile that gives the hiring manager a glimpse of your skill and accomplishments. It includes employment skills such as teamwork, problem solving initiative, planning, organising and self management.
- **Personal Information** This part covers about the DOB, marital status etc of the candidate
- **Hobbies and Interest** This will help the employer to know about your likes and dislikes, personality etc. As your hobbies also reflects your inner personality.
- **Salary Drawn and Salary Expected** You have to be very careful during writing the information regarding salary drawn and expectation. You are required to give this type of information only in case of requirement of the employer. Otherwise you can simply write in this column as "My salary requirement is negotiable based upon the job responsibilities and the total compensation package".
- **References** The purpose of including references in resume is to validate your given information by the employer for references, you can use the name of teacher or professor, who has known you well, a former employer if possible or any other person who is well known.

Important Points to be Kept in Mind While Writing Resume

- First and foremost thing, one must keep in mind, for what job he/she applying for, so focus on qualities that match for the requirement of that organisation.
- Mention your career objective clearly and avoid confusing and common phrases. Avoid unnecessary personal details such as age, religion etc.
- List your career and educational qualification details in reverse chronological order. Include computer skills, language skills and any relevant training. Keep the hobbies and interest section short.
- Mention your contact details carefully. Last but not the least do not copy from other's resume, it may ruin all your achievements.

ELECTRONIC RESUME

In the age of electronics, companies are processing job applicants at incredibly high speeds. While the format chosen and the words appearing on a resume are important, it is equally important that the document can be effectively scanned into a database. By switching to an electronic format, employees working in the human resources department can now quickly match job applicants to open positions within the organisation.

Some tips for writing electronic resume are given below

- **Use a Plain Font** While writing electronic resume one must remember to use plain font size. One should never mix different font types or font sizes for data. One must use a standard serif type face such as courier Times, Arial, Verdana or Franklin Gothic.
- **Never Use PDF** The resume should be in Microsoft 'Word format'. Recruiters want resumes in Microsoft Word. If one is not able to use Microsoft Word, use RTF or "Save as Text" instead.
- **Do not use Graphics to Represent Data** Graphics (clip art, photos, Logos etc) should be ignored. Many times people put important contact data into a graphic. This data is invisible to passing software, so their resume is useless.
- **Do not use Tables or Multi Column Formats** Tables are neat and pretty to humans. Unfortunately most document conversion software cannot handle tables and will either scramble the text into an undecipherable words or it will space the data with extra lines that may confuse the software.
- **Use Capital Letters for Headings** While writing the section headers, capital letters should be used. One must write one's name, employer's name, job title, school names, degree names, locations (city, region, country) etc in capital letters.
- **Use Nothing Smaller than 10 Point Type** The resume should be written in such a manner that employer may not need any magnifying glass. Also don't expect readers to struggle through 10-15 line paragraphs. Substitute two or three shorter paragraph or use bullets to offset new sentences and sections.
- **Do not Clutter your Resume** Let your document 'breathe'. So, readers or prospective employers won't have to struggle through it. Type all your information starting on the left hand side of the page. Don't centre or justify any text. These formating commands don't transmit well electronically. One should use a second page rather than pack everything into one page and have it scan unclearly.

Sample Resume

Resume for Marketing Manager

SUMIT VIZ
House No. 475, Panampalli Nagar
Kochin, Kerala
Mobile no. **********
email-sumit12@gmail.com

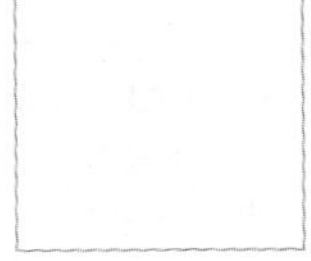

Career Objective

Seeking a management position where my leadership, strategic planning and business development skills will be fully utilised.

Educational Background

- Masters of Business Administration fropm IIM Calcutta in the year 2010.
- BA Hons. (Economics) from Madurai Kamraj University in the year 2008.

Computer Skills

- Operating Systems Window 2000, Windows XP, Windows Vista, Linux, MS DOS
- Office Package Microsoft Word, Excel, Powerpoint, Access.

Professional Skills

- Expertise in strategic planning, budgeting/finance, customer service and staff training, supervision and mentoring.
- Excellent leadership, management, oral/written communication, interpersonal, intuitive and analysis skill.
- Energetic and self-motivated team player. Able to handle stress situation with ease.
- Comfortable in fast paced environments with emerging multiple responsibilities.

Work Experience

- Star Corporation, At post of Sales Assistant Manager from May 2013 to present

- Managed day to day operations, supervised and coordinated activities of employees.
- Improved productivity and morale by initiating effective training programmes and inculcating accountability.
- Planned, prepared and devised work schedules, according to budgets and work loads.
- Developed new strategies to meet customer expectations.

Achievements

- Best Achiever Award from the Company.
- Power Corporation, Chennai, At post of Manager from May 2011 to January 2013
- Successfully handled customer and employee complaints before reaching upper management.
- Recorded data for each employee including such information as absences, amount of sales and production and supervisory reports on performance.
- Submitted and reviewed reports and problems with higher management.

Personal Information

- Date of Birth : 8 August 1987
- Marital Status : Single

Languages Known

- Hindi, English, Spanish

Hobbies and Interests

- Travelling and reading novels

Salary Expected

Negotiable

Declaration

I hereby declare that the above mentioned information is correct up to my knowledge and I bear the responsibility for the correctness of the above mentioned particulars.

Date ________

Place ________

Resume for the Post of Sales Executive

NAVEEN DWIVEDI
C-5, Vasant Kunj, New Delhi
Mobile no. **********
email naveen24@yahoo.com

Career Objective

Prove to be an important asset for a reputed organisation where I could utilise my skills and competencies to the utmost level.

Educational Qualifications

- B.Com. Hons. from Mumbai University
- XII from Maharashtra Board
- X from Maharashtra Board

Academic Projects

Project 1 Sales and promotion of a new product launched in the market.

- Strategising the sales and advertising techniques.
- Finalising the target market and promoting the product.
- Taking reviews of the people who have already used that particular product.

Key Skills

- Conversational skills
- Interpersonal skills
- Presentation skills
- Technical skills
- Microsoft Office
- Extracurricular Activities
- Participated in a seminar on 'The Methods of Advertising'
- Participated in inter school quiz

Personal Information

- Date of Birth-10 March 1990
- Maritial Status-Single

Hobbies and Interest

- Travelling new places around India. Playing squash

Languages known

- English, Hindi, Marathi

Salary Expected

Negotiable

Declaration

I hereby declare that the informtion furnished about is true to the best of my knowledge.

Date ________

Place ________

Resume for the Post of Lecturer

SHILPA DHAWAN
489, C-5
Vasant Kunj
Mobile no. **********
New Delhi

Career Objective

- Seeking the position of an teacher in your institution, will give me an opportunity to pass on my knowledge to the students in an innovative manner.
- Offer support and well disciplined environment to ensure the success of each and every child.

Professional Profile

Responsible elementary school teacher with excellent communication skills, demonstrated by 9 years of teaching experience. Passion for education, especially science education for children. Motivated, energetic, enthusiastic education with a strong desire to foster a proper student learning atmosphere. Experienced in managing students effectively and maximising learning opportunities in diverse classroom settings.

Educational Qualifications

	Academic University	Year	Degree	Marks
1.	Jamia Milia University	2008	M. Ed. (Science)	80% marks
2.	Jamia Milia University	2006	B. Ed. Edu.	78% marks
3.	Delhi University	2004	B. Sc. Hons.	82% marks

Professional/Teaching Experience

4th Grade Teacher

- Bhatnagar International School, Vasant Kunj, from July 2011 to till today.
- Develop interesting course plans to meet academic intellectual and social needs of students.
- Co-ordination after school tutoring hours with other teachers to help students in need of extra attention.
- Applied progressive teaching principles to a class of 29 students, improving standardised test scores.
- Received high remarks for the creativity of classroom lesson plans and instructional techniques from students, parents and faculty.

2nd Grade Teacher

- Bloom Public School, C-8 Vasant Kunj, from April 2009 to May 2011.
- Developed, administered tests and quizzes in a timely manner.
- Implemented interesting and interactive learning mediums to increase student's understanding of course-materials.
- Performed student background reviews to develop tailored lessons based on student's needs.
- Lessons planned to increase student's concentration, participation and progress student's accountability.

Extracurricular Activities

- Have taken part in inter college debates and quizzes.
- Fond of reading novels and magazines.

Personal Information

- Date of Birth : 11 September 1989
- Marital Status : Single

Salary Expected

Negotiable

Declaration

I hereby declare that the above mentioned information is correct to my knowledge and I bear the responsibility for the correctness of the above mentioned particulars.

Date ______

Place ______

Resume for the Post of Chartered Accountant

SHAILESH BANNERJEE
H. no. 489, C-5
Mobile no.
Mail id - bannerjee199@gmail.com
Address - P-5, Anupam apartments, Saket, New-Delhi

Career Objective

Would like to start my career as Chartered Accountant with a well-established organisation to contribute in growth by using my accountancy skills and legal knowledge.

Professional Key Skills

- Strong analytical and problem solving skills.
- Excellent knowledge in handling accounting system.
- Well versed in using an automated accounting system.
- Excellent communication skills.
- Full and high energy and motivation.

Educational Background

- Passed 5 years CA programme from Institute of Chartered Accountant.
- Ranked 12th (All India) in the G.A. foundation examination. From institution of chartered Accountants Lodhi Road.
- B.Com. Hons. from Delhi University, Hindu College 80% marks.
- Senior Secondary (CBSE) Amity School, Saket, New Delhi 85% marks.

Work Experience

Two years work experience in a CA firm 'Mittal and Associates' Connaught Place, New Delhi while doing CA course.

Key Learning Areas

- Assisting the senior CA in his working.
- Learning about the company laws.
- Assisted in company and individual's tax filing.
- Learning about professional tax assessment and submission of returns.
- Three months training from 'Vashist Capitals' on cost sheet and profit and loss management.

Projects

- **Profit and Loss Study** This project was about complete study of five IT companies and to study about their profit and loss statement.

Extra Curricular Activities and Hobbies

- Helped in school audit.
- Participated in inter school quiz competitions.
- Fond of playing badminton.
- Watching English movies.

Personal Details

- Date of Birth : 0.1.02.1988
- Marital Status : Single

Languages known

- Hindi, English, Bengali

Hobbies and Interests

- Reading Novels, Travelling

Expected Salary

Negotiable

Declaration

I hereby declare that the above mentioned information is correct to my knowledge and I hear the responsibility for the correctness of the above mentioned particulars.

Date _________

Place _________

Resume for the Post of Computer Engineer

ASHWINI MAURYA
H. no. 391/1
Mobile no. **********
E mail ID Ashwin01@yahoo.com

Career Objectives

- A hardworking professional with excellent analytical, logical skills, perform in highly demanding atmosphere. Able to develop various programmes on different languages for existing software.
- Excellent data reporting skills using software as well as statistical methods.

Personal Skills

- Unmatchable communication skills in verbal and written both.
- Excellent analytical and logical skills.
- Ability to work individually as well as in a team.

Technical Knowledge

- Excellent in MS office (MS Word, MS Excel, MS Power point)
- Proficient in C, Java, PHP and MYSQL.
- Well versed in Macromedia, Bugzilla and Photoshop.
- Skiled in designing, programming and testing.

Key Responsibilities Handled

- Suggest innovative ideas to enhance the working of existing software.
- Finding the problems and suggest the best possible solution.
- Presenting the model in front of seniors and elaborate it.
- Perform various duties as assigned.

Achievements

- Gave a presentation of 'Software Science' at ERT University.
- Made the hacking software for SDF solutions.
- Receive 'Best Employees' award in 2011.

Employers

- Working as software engineer in ACL Company from April 2013 till now.
- Worked as Software Assistant Engineer in Genpact company from January 2009 to February 2013.

Educational Qualifications

- Masters in Computer Science Engineering from Jaipur University in 2008.
- B.Tech in Computer Science Engineering for Jaipur University in 2006.
- B.Sc from D.A.V. College, Udaipur in 2003.
- Senior Secondary (CBSE) from Paul Foundations Udaipur, Rajasthan in 2000.

Personal Details

- Date of Birth : 27th July, 1987
- Marital status : Married

Languages known

- English, Hindi

Hobbies and Interest

- Internet surfing, listening music

Expected Salary

- Negotiable

Declaration

I hereby declare that the above mentioned information is correct to my knowledge and I hear the responsibility for the correctness of the above mentioned particulars.

Date ________

Place ________

Resume for the Post of Senior IT Analyst

PRATIK SHARMA
H. No. 99112
Mobile no. **********
E mail ID Pratik04@yahoo.com

Career Objectives

Award-winning, detail-focused and result-oriented IT professional with comprehensive system support and ugrading, troubleshooting and effective training experience. Dedicated, organised, and self-directed team member with a keen eye on the bottom line and strong relationship-building and communication skills.

Specialisation Skills

- System Analysis Data collection, evaluating, proposing solution
- Web Development Programming, graphic design, relational database management.
- Project Management Understanding SDLC methodology, effective negotiations, project delivery.
- IT Compliance Systems Audit, disaster recovery coordination.

Technical Skills

- Languages HTML, DHTML, Java, Java Script, ASP, SQL, Visual Basic 6.0, Loutus Notes R5
- Platforms Window 2000/XP, Internet Information Services
- Software Microsoft Office Suite, Project Vision, Visual SourceSafe, SQL Server 2000.

Achievements

- Six Sigma Green Belt, Johnson Process Excellence
- Systematic Project Managment Certification, Johnson and Johnson Services Consortium
- Member, Information Systems Audit and Control Association

Work Experience

- ABC Incorporated, Noida
- As IT Analyst lead support and administrator for the Siebel Advantis Plus program, a hospital case management application used by 100 + professional education specialists nationwide. Minimise technical issues, and provide timely updates and training. Direct product life-cycle management, Global Complaint System and client-server based applications as database and system administrator.

- Audited a JDE One World system at another Johnson and Johnson company, in the areas of application security, CNC, and OMW, as part of Guest Auditor Program, identified and communicated potential security holes and presented recommendations to senior management.
- Recognised by the audit manger for successful completion of audit work.
- Utilised the hands-on experience of the Guest Auditor Program to complete a mock audit of JDE OneWorld system at Biosense Webster. Identified improper configuration and excess privileges; recommendations to resolve the problems were approved by the IT and Finance Directors and implemented.
- ABC Enterprises Bengaluru
- Worked as IT associate analyst, technical lead for the implementation of accounts, recievable management software project in the Finance Department. Ensured hardware and software compliance and compatibility, converted and mapped data from existing financial system to be operable with new system.

Personal Information

- Date of Birth : 11th November, 1987
- Marital status : Single

Languages known

Hindi, English, French

Hobbies and Interest

Mountain trekking, listening music

Salary Expected

Negotiable

Declaration

I hereby declare that the above mentioned information is correct to my knowledge and I hear the responsibility for the correctness of the above mentioned particulars.

Date ________

Place ________

COVER LETTER

A cover letter is a document sent with resume to provide additional information of one's skills and experiences. While writing cover letter one should take care to write a cover letter effectively and in impressive manner. The content and format of the cover letters vary according to the position and the qualification of the candidate.

Before writing cover letter one should keep in mind that cover letter should be a compliment to his/her resume but not duplicate. Effective cover letter mentions the reasons why one is interested in particular organisation and is unique and fit for the post.

Effective and impressive cover letter must include outlines i.e. beginning, middle and conclusion part. The beginning should be used to arouse interest at the out set. Your letter should be simple, brief and to the point. In the middle paragraph, try to reemphasise briefly specific achievements and work experience. Closing of a covering letter is equally important. Concluding paragraph should be to ensure the desired result getting an interview call.

Check List for Covering Letter

- Your letter should be correctly dated.
- Write your correct mailing address with proper format.
- Check the receiver's address before putting the letter in mail-box.
- Do not forget to sign the letter.
- Ensure there is no grammatical error or spelling mistakes.
- Indicate at the end of covering letter the list of enclosures
  e.g. Encl : Resume

SAMPLE COVER LETTER

ANEES GYANI
H. no. **********
Mobile no. **********
email-abc@gmail.com

12th November, 2016

DEVYANI MAHAJAN
Hiring Manager
SFL Ltd.
Sector 55
Noida (U.P)

Dear Miss Mahajan,

It is with great interest that I am applying for the position of AVP accounts in your organisation as advertised in Economic Times dated 7th November, 2016. I possess about 5 years experience in construction and contracting domain. I believe I am suitable for the job advertised by you.

With excellent knowledge of financial service industry. I am currently pursuing ACCA which has helped keep myself, updated with the latest financial trends.

As demonstration of my seriousness and commitment to the job quest, I have been prescreened by an online background verification service with the report available for review. My past employer can attest my abilities to use my financial and accounting expertise to take on a management and leadership role in the business.

Enclosed please find my detailed resume which highlights my qualification and work experience. Please feel free to contact me by phone or e-mail.

Thank you for your time and consideration. I look forward to be called for an interview.

Best Regards

ANEES GYANI

FAQ

Commonly asked Questions During An INTERVIEW

Some Common Questions are generally asked in the interview. Here, we are providing you some questions which will help you in preparing your base level. By answering these basic questions in a smart way, one can secure the highest chances of selection.

QUESTIONS TO BREAK THE ICE

Tell me about yourself.

*(**Our comment** This may be meant for exposing your bad habits/weaknesses.)*

- Only discuss what your interests are relating to the job you are being interviewed for and why your background makes you a great candidate. The interviewers are definitely not interested in your life story.

What made you apply for this job/post?

*(**Our comment** This question is asked to find out immediately what kind of research the candidate has done to prepare for the interview.)*

- You should be able to competently discuss the employer's area of operation, the reputation of the organisation and any recent activity that has been made public. You should be able to match your strengths and values with the needs of the organisation.

How did you prepare for this interview?

*(**Our comment** This question is asked to find out how much the applicant really cares about the job opportunity. Employers want to hire people committed to going above and beyond the call of duty, even when preparing for interviews.)*

- When replying to such questions, you should emphasise your desire for the job before specifically describing each step taken to prepare for the interview process. You should have gone through the organisation website before the interview and learnt enough about the employer to demonstrate adequate preparation and interest in job.

What are your strengths?

- Talk about your strengths; for instance, you are detail oriented, hard working, a team player etc.

What are your weaknesses?

- It's easy to get tripped up when discussing your weaknesses. Never talk about a real weakness unless it's something you've been able to overcome. An example is that you used to reach late to work often, but after your supervisor explained why it was necessary for you to come on time, you were never late again.

QUESTIONS BASED ON EDUCATION AND INTEREST

Why do you want to enter this job?

*(**Our comment** Usually, this is for freshers or people switching from one line of work to another. The interviewers want to find out how enthusiastic you are about your choice or what inspires you and that you have a rationale for entering a particular profession.)*

- As everyone likes to be flattered, so one should tell them what he or she likes about the company, tell them that you are ready to face challenges and passionate to work with them, emphasise what you can contribute and mention your skills and work experience to show that you are strong and unique for the job.

What was your favourite subject in school and why?

*(**Our comment** The interviewer is trying to understand why you like and what you like.)*

- You can use such a question as an opportunity to talk about an achievement or award you got. For instance, if you say that your favourite subject is English, you can speak about a writing competition that you won. This is a good trigger question that you can expand to bring your impressive achievements into the conversation with the interviewer. While employer asks you such question anything you mention should be related directly to the position you are applying for.

Which is your favourite book?

*(**Our comment** What the interviewer really wants to learn is who you are. What you say about the importance of reading the book is indicative of your interests, beliefs, goals, likes and dislikes.)*

- Don't give a complete book review when you answer this question. When thinking about which book to choose, ask yourself if your selection made you think differently or compelled you to take a certain action. Ask yourself what specifically made you relate to a particular character. Also don't feel that you have to select a classic–any book will do. What's important is not your book choice but why it is meaningful to you.

Why did you opt for a government/bank job when, with your qualifications, you can easily get a much better salaried job in the private sector?

*(**Our comment** Usually, by asking this type of questions interviewes wants to know how interested you are in bank job and the may also ask you this question to make you speak about your clarity of thoughts.*

- Do not say that there is job security in government / bank jobs which is not there in private sector jobs, because it will show that you lack self-confidence or have a negative attitude.

You can mention that, as a government / bank employee, you will be serving the people as well as contributing to the growth of the nation. *(If you have your relative or parents etc associated with these jobs you can cite the example of such cases saying that you are inspired by them.)*

Which is your favourite website?

*(**Our comment** The interviewer wants to know about who you are and how you spend your free time. The question can give insight into what your passions are and how much time you spend on self-improvement.)*

- Unless it is relevant to the position, do not include social media like Facebook, Linked in etc. Do not choose a website that you know nothing about. Try to mention a site that combines professionalism and entertainment value.

When discussing why you like the site, incorporate positive character traits such as an interest in learning new skills. Focus your answer on how the site supports self-improvement.

A typical answer may be, "My favourite website is HowStuffWorks.com because it combines humour with the educational topics it informs about. I love to laugh, but I want to stay informed about the world and its latest social and scientific advancements. This website can deliver learning with a touch of humour."

What are your hobbies?

Or What do you do in your spare time?

*(**Our comment** The interviewer is interested in knowing your overall health and energy level, your mentality. Hobbies best reflect your strengths passions and skills and helps the interviewer to evaluate you as a perfect fit for the job.*

- If your favourite way to pass time is gambling, partying, or any type of illegal or questionable activity, don't bring it up in the interview. Also, do not mention 'listening to music', 'reading' etc, as these are too vague.

Instead, try to give examples that demonstrate a positive quality that might indirectly help you to achieve success at work, like exercise and health-related activities, volunteering, participation in social service of the community, professional development, continuing education etc.

QUESTIONS BASED ON CURRENT AND PREVIOUS POSITIONS

Why do you want to leave your present job/company?

*(**Our comment** This will be asked to know that you either have positive or negative attitude about your previous boss or job.)*

- If you want to leave the present company because you don't like your boss, don't talk negatively about him. Instead, say that you have a different work philosophy than him. If the work was boring to you, just mention that you're looking for a more challenging position.

Discuss the positive points that are in your most recent job and focus on why you think the new position would be ideal for you and how the new company will benefit from your joining.

Why have you left your last employer?

*(**Our comment** This will be asked only if you have mentioned that you are no longer employed.)*

- You may have left your employer due to either being laid off, being terminated (also called 'fired') or left of your own accord.

In each case, the reply will have to be different :

- **Laid off** Tell them that you were let go, and that you understand the circumstances behind their decision; that you are committed to your future and ready to apply everything that you learned in your last job in a new organisation.
- **Terminated** Do not criticise your last boss or organisation. Tell them that you were unfortunately let go, that you understand their reasoning and you've recognised areas that you need to improve in and explain how you will be a better employee because of it.
- **Left of your own accord** Do not go into details about your unhappiness or dissatisfaction. Instead, tell them that while you valued the experience and education that you received, you felt that the time had come to seek out a new opportunity, to expand your skills and knowledge and to find an organisation with which you could grow.

What are your three positive qualities that your last boss may mention about you?

***(Our comment** The interviewer is trying to find out what your strong points are and how you prioritise them. He gives you chance to use the words of others to talk about your positive qualities.)*

- Do not go to the interview unprepared for such a question. You should know what your best qualities are. Also, do not read from your bio-data. Your answers should be more personal than the qualities you put on your bio-data. Do not exaggerate or boast about your qualities. Experienced interviewers will catch your boast.

Try to be unique, honest and specific about your qualities. An ideal answer could be, "In my previous job, I had a strong reputation as the knowledgeable employee. Other employees would almost use me as an encyclopaedia. I also never had any trouble meeting time constraints. I was never late or missed a deadline. My last quality which my boss might mention is that I dealt very well with customers."

What were your boss' strengths/ weaknesses in the previous job?

***(Our comment** This question is a sign that you are being considered seriously for the job. It tests your loyalty and your honesty by checking to see how you will approach the issue and it also allows the interviewer to determine how objective and evidence-based your judgement is.)*

- Do not attack your previous boss. Make sure that you answer the strength part of the question, no matter how you might feel personally about the boss. Similarly, you should avoid evaluating the boss based on his personal habits or peculiarities which don't affect the job. A good answer would be something like, "In my last job, my supervisor was good at informing about the work process and timing, but conflict resolution was a bit of a problem with him.

If two departments had a conflict, he rarely intervened to settle the issue, so the resolution of the conflict was delayed. It gave individual workers more chance to be heard, but I'm not sure I'd let things go on so long if it was me; however, I would certainly make sure I heard everyone before speaking up."

BEHAVIOURAL QUESTIONS

How have you been a leader or displayed leadership?

***(Our comment** By asking this question interviewer wants to find out true leadership potential of the candidate whether he can work as a team or not.)*

- Don't only list the titles and positions you have held. Instead, focus on a specific leadership position or activity and give enough detail to show the depth of your commitment by citing concrete accomplishments in that position.

Are you willing to relocate/shift from the town where you work currently for the job?

*(**Our comment** The interviewer wants to understand your flexibility and whether you are not tied down to your current home. Also understand that if you refuse, you may lose the job.)*

- A formal answer would be: "For the right opportunity I am definitely willing to relocate. I believe that this position and organisation is that opportunity." You can also say," Yes, sir, I will be happy with the relocation because I will be able to meet new people and new cultures. Learning is a never-ending process, whether it could mean learning a new subject or meeting new people and places. So, I am okay with relocation."

Are you willing to travel during the job?

*(**Our comment** The interviewer wants to see that you understand the role of travel in the normal function of a company.)*

- When you answer this question, you want to show that you are not opposed to the idea of travel. An excellent answer to this question may be: "I am ready to travel for doing my work. Travel in my previous jobs has allowed me to go to special conferences and trainings that have expanded my knowledge. Travel is required in many cases to network and complete job responsibilities. I always like to be an asset to the company for which I work." Never complain about or talk about past misfortunes at airports or railway stations. Be careful not to explain that you enjoy sight-seeing or going on vacation.

What motivates you?

*(**Our comment** This question is very broad and easy to misinterpret. Interviewer wants to know what do you think, what your values, are you fit for the post etc.)*

- The best answers to these questions are to be honest and yet should also relate to the skills and aptitudes required for the job you are being interviewed for. Whatever you say, you need to back it up with examples from your studies, work experience and/or extracurricular activities.

You can say something like, "I'm motivated by visible results; for instance, when I wrote an article for my university magazine, I felt a sense of accomplishment from knowing that upto 6000 students would read it."

Are you a leader or a follower?

*(**Our comment** This is a trap question, as interviewer is finding a versatile candidate and willing to find a person who can play different role based on company's requirement.)*

- Your answer should combine a little of both. Tilt your answer towards what is required in the job you are being interviewed for. If it is an entry level job, don't focus too heavily on being a leader. If it is a management job, prepare to answer the most common management questions and focus less on being a follower. A good answer will be, "I adapt my working style to the position I am in. When a group needs a leader, I gladly take on that role, but at entry level, I know that there is a lot I need to learn, and I am happy to take direction from those with more knowledge and experience."

Tell us about an accomplishment you are most proud of.

*(**Our comment** Your description of the achievement helps the interviewer evaluate whether your skills and character traits are a good fit for the position in question. This can help the interviewer decide whether your personal attitudes would fit well with the organisation's culture and objectives.)*

- Do not undermine your accomplishment by trying to act modest or provide a simple and short answer that won't help the interviewer understand you. Don't mention an achievement having no relevance to the job and don't exaggerate a real accomplishment or fabricate one that you think will sound impressive. Instead, provide detailed information to establish your credibility and help the interviewer understand the value of your accomplishment. A typical answer would be , "My biggest accomplishment is completing my Bachelors degree with a high Grade Point Average (GPA). I am proud of it because it took a lot of dedication, diligence and self-control to always put my studies before anything else."

Would you work on holidays/weekends?

*(**Our comment** This question tests your flexibility.)*

- Do not forget to account for the nature of the organisation, as some bank employees may have to work odd hours. Do not commit to a schedule that you will not be able to maintain while not hiding other time consuming obligations. Even if you think your response is not what the interviewer is looking for, it is better to be honest than to find yourself ultimately working more or less than you wanted. A typical answer may be, "I'm an efficient worker, though I will gladly put in extra time, when needed, if I find that I cannot get the vast majority of my work tasks completed during the regular working week. Thus, I have no problem with the occasional long work weekend or working on a holiday when necessary."

What makes you uncomfortable?

*(**Our comment** The interviewer is trying to find out how you handle difficult moments and whether these moments affect your overall job performance. By demonstrating an ability to remain cool under pressure and address the problem, you'll impress him.)*

- Focus on one incident and give a real-life example. Talking about one main discomfort will give you a chance to show how you identified the problem and the steps you took to resolve it. A typical answer will be, "I'm uncomfortable in situations where matters are disorganised. I always try to organise matters when I come across such a situation. Recently, in a group project which was initially disorganised, I outlined everyone's responsibilities and streamlined our workflow. We went from not being sure of our roles to getting everything done very efficiently, and we were able to actually finish the project earlier than the target date."

Give us an example of a time when you had a problem with a supervisor / co-worker and how you approached the problem / solved the problem.

*(**Our comment** This is a key question for selection. Interviewer's perspective is to find out about candidate's conflict management ability and inter-personal skills to handle tense situation.)*

- Most employees have a problem with a supervisor or co-worker at some point in their career. How they handle that problem says a lot about their people management skills (also known as 'soft skills'). If you can explain to the interviewer how you were able to overcome a problem at work, this will definitely help your chances of getting the job.

Tell me about a time you made a mistake.

*(**Our comment** The interviewer wants to know whether you are a person who can learn from failure and are you self-aware enough to acknowledge failure or a weakness.)*

- Never say something like: "Well, I can't think of any serious failures. I guess I've been fortunate to be pretty successful in most of my positions so far." You should prepare a suitable failure story before you go for the interview, in case such a question is asked. Typical answers should highlight your strengths by focusing on what happened after the mistake occurred. Discuss the mistake in a manner that shows that you feel a sense of accountability. Describe what action you took to correct the mistake when you became aware of it. Explain the proactive measures that you now use to avoid similar mistakes. Explain what you have learnt from the experience. Try to take a positive approach that shows the interviewer you are committed to learning and improving your work.

How would you deal with an angry or irate customer?

*(**Our comment** This question is usually asked in marketing, servicing and jobs that involve dealing with the public.)*

- Your response to this question must show how well you were able to remain in control of the entire interaction between you and the irate customer. The ideal answer will be something like this: "Sometimes customers may be upset or unhappy with their experience with a particular product or service and will contact the company to let them know. I would acknowledge their feelings and concerns and inform them that I would be more than happy to assist them by resolving the problem. After exhausting all available resources, if I could not rectify the situation, I would let the customer know that I can put them in touch with a supervisor who can help them if necessary."

Tell us about a time when your workload was very heavy. How did you manage it?

***(Our comment** Here the interviewer is looking for a person who plans his work in advance, not doing the work as it comes to him.)*

- You can answer something like, "Last year, I had to manage two departments because one department head had left the job. So, I made a day planner in advance for every week and mapped all my work on it, dividing the total working time into suitable compartments. Thus, I could finish the work of both departments in the given time."

How do you handle pressure in your job?

***(Our comment** This question is usually asked in bank jobs and in marketing / servicing jobs that involve dealing with the public.)*

- You can answer something like, "I react to situations, rather than to pressure or stress. That way, the situation is handled and doesn't become stressful" or you can say, "I'm the kind of person who stays calm under pressure and handles stress comfortably by prioritising my actions and working accordingly." You should be ready to give examples of the past when you have handled pressure. That way, the interviewers will get a clear picture how well you can work in stressful situations.

BRAIN TEASERS OR TRICKY QUESTIONS

Where do you see yourself five years from now?

***(Our comment** This actually means "Is this job even close to your presumed career path?" or "Are you just applying for this job because you need some job?")*

- Explain to them that you've done some self-assessment and career planning. Let them know that you hope to develop professionally and take on additional responsibilities at that particular company in future. Don't say something like, "I don't know" or "I want your job."

If Bill Gates walked into your office and offered you one million dollars to launch your best business idea, what would it be?

- Think about what significance the question might have to the job you are applying for and what you have already informed the interviewers about your interests (if you have done so). Also understand that the business idea should be related to computers, software or other related businesses. It should also relate to something which is much in demand currently. Do not mention social service (with which Bill Gates is actively involved currently) as that is not a business but a service to humanity. Accordingly frame your answer.

How much salary do you expect or What are your salary requirements?

*(**Our comment** What the interviewer wants to know is, 'Do you have realistic expectations when it comes to salary?' or 'Do you want much more than we can give?' or 'Are you flexible on this point or is your expectation fixed?')*

- If you are being interviewed for a job like Probationary Officer/ Management Trainee / any other job with an advertised and known stipend or scale pay, you can say that the stipend or salary is all right with you. In such a case, work out before attending the interview the actual total amount you will be paid. If the interviewer asks about the amount, you can state the worked out amount.

However, if the salary is not fixed and is negotiable, take your experience and education levels into consideration, as well as the location where you will work. For instance, if you have to work in Mumbai, Delhi or any other metropolitan city, you will require a higher salary than if you were posted in a district town or rural area. Mention the range of salary, not a specific amount. Also mention that you are flexible in this and that you're open to considering benefits as well.

Why should we hire you?

- Every question you answer in the interview should contribute to helping them understand why you're the best person for the job. Stay focused on why your background makes you an ideal candidate and tell them how you are going to contribute to that department and that organisation.

How would you feel about working under someone who knows less than you or is less qualified than you?

*(**Our comment** The interviewer is trying to find out whether you understand that there are people who know more than you and you can learn something from them.)*

- Even if you can't learn something from them, then help them to be successful which will result in your success. A good answer may be, "I believe that there isn't just one type of knowledge. For instance, someone can be theoretically knowledgeable and another can be practically smart. I think the best supervisor/ workman relationship is where both people balance each other out and where they both feel that there are things they can learn from each other."

Other candidates are more qualified/experienced than you for this job. Then why should we give you this job?

- Do not compare yourself to or discuss about other candidates. Try to convince the interviewers only about how you are suitable. You can say, "I don't know about other candidates, but I'm adequately qualified and experienced for this job. I am fully confident of carrying out my duties successfully."

INFORMATION AND OPINION BASED QUESTIONS

What are your career goals?

*(**Our comment** The interviewer is trying to make sure that your goals are in line with what you would be doing in the new job. They want to make sure that you won't leave the job soon after joining. This question also helps them determine if you are a good fit for the department / bank / organisation.)*

- Do not mention a career path that could not happen in the organisation / job you are being interviewed for. Don't give a feeble or weak answer.

Be careful not to boast about what you think you will achieve.

Instead, keep your answer positive, concise and in line with what the organisation does.

This will show the interviewer just how much you want to work for them. Your answer could be, "My current goals include staying up-to-date, which means I will attend seminars and workshops when possible. I also want to use the knowledge that I gain to help others reach their top potential. I see myself in the future as being a great leader and manager who pushes the employees to excel and therefore make the organisation better."

What is your dream job?

*(**Our comment** The interviewer is interested in how motivated you are to perform the job and whether or not you will be satisfied with the job. This interview question helps him assess your motivation.)*

- If your real dream job has nothing to do with the job you're being interviewed for, don't mention it. You should make an effort to connect your answer to the job you're being interviewed for. For instance, if the job is a customer service/dealing with the public type of job, you may say that your dream job would have a high level of interaction with customers.

You completed your last qualification about a year ago. What were you doing since then, as this is not mentioned in your bio-data?

- Never say that you were doing nothing. Say something like, "Besides preparing for the written test and interview for this job, I had taken up a job as a part-time teacher in an evening college. This helped me to earn some money while I was preparing."

Why do you want to leave your present job in the private sector, as the job with us is paying less?

*(**Our comment** This question is often asked if a person already employed in private sector is now being interviewed for a government / bank job.)*

- Do not say that there is job security in government / bank jobs which is not there in private sector jobs, because it will show that you lack self-confidence or have a negative attitude. You may say that in the current job, the future prospects are very poor, or you can say that the current job is very routine and you are looking for a challenging opportunity to use your skills and training.

Where do you see yourself in five years?

- Our comment (If asked this question, be honest and specific about you future goals) you can answer something like this 'Well I'm really excited by this position at 'Midnight Consulting' because in five years, I'd like to be seen as someone with deep expertise in the energy sector, and I know that's something that I will have an opportunity to do here. I' m also really excited to take on more managerial responsibilities in the next few years and potentially even take the lead on some projects. I've been lucky enough to work with some amazing managers, and so developing into a great manager myself is something I'm really excited about.